DISCOVERING

PURPOSE, CALLING & GIFTS

DISCIPLING NATIONS SERIES #2
ABRAHAM JOHN

DISCOVERING PURPOSE, CALLING, AND GIFTS
DISCIPLING NATIONS SERIES # 2

Copyright © 2020 by Abraham John

Published by Abraham John

www.TheKingdomNetwork.org
email: info@thekingdomnetwork.org
1-800-558-5020

ISBN: 978-1-948330-19-0

Printed in the United States of America

Unless otherwise indicated, all Scripture is taken from the New King James Version®. Copyright © 1982 by Thomas Nelson. Used by permission.

Scripture marked (KJV) is from the King James Bible, which is in the public domain.

Scripture quotations marked (NLT) are taken from the Holy Bible, New Living Translation, copyright © 1996, 2004, 2015 by Tyndale House Foundation. Used by permission of Tyndale House Publishers, Inc., Carol Stream, Illinois 60188. All rights reserved.

Scripture quotations marked (KJV) are from the King James Version and are in the public domain.

All emphases or additions in parentheses within scriptural quotations are the author's own. All rights reserved. No part of this book may be reproduced or transmitted in any form or by any means, electronic or mechanical, including photocopying, recording, or by any information storage and retrieval system, without permission in writing from the author. Please direct your inquiries to info@thekingdomnetwork.org

CONTENTS

Preface 5

Introduction 9

Chapter 1: Three Biggest Lies I Was Taught 13

Chapter 2: Understanding Salvation 19

Chapter 3: Understanding Worship 27

Chapter 4: Understanding Purpose 45

Chapter 5: The Purpose, Power, and Function of Mankind 55

Chapter 6 ; The Six-Fold Eternal Purposes of Mankind 71

Chapter 7: Our Original Assignment 85

Chapter 8: The Law of Dominion 97

Chapter 9: Twelve Definitions of Dominion 113

Chapter 10: Nine Ways to Have Dominion 127

Chapter 11: The Process of Taking and Exercising Dominion 135

Chapter 12: The Purpose, Power, and Function of Israel ... 147

Chapter 13: The Purpose, Power, and Function of the Church 159

Chapter 14: Calling –The Key to Fulfilling Your Purpose .. 177

Chapter 15: Gifts: The Key to Fulfilling Your Calling 191

Chapter 16: Seven Reasons for Poverty 203

Chapter 17: Discipling Nations–True Discipleship 207

Genesis126 Project 229

More Books & Resources 235

PREFACE

Throughout the centuries, all great preachers and philosophers taught that each one of us has a unique purpose. There is a great deal written and spoken about this subject, but the majority of people alive on this earth today are clueless about their purpose. Most of the people I meet in life are confused and wondering why they are here.

I often meet people of all ages that say this: "I don't know what am I supposed to do with my life." People have invented many methods and techniques to help people discover their purpose, but the truth is that 93% of them are not sure why they are here, or what they are supposed to do with their life. They are all in survival mode.

Thousands of seminars and conferences have been held on the subject of purpose. Millions and billions of dollars have been spent on people trying to discover the reason for their existence. It has been a hot topic in our day and in every generation. The business world calls it finding our "big why." In truth, we will keep questioning the reason for our existence in every new season of our life.

Every religion has tried to come up with an answer for their followers about their purpose, but none could figure out a solution that gave real meaning and hope to people. Many are still wandering in the dark, looking for the meaning of life. Most have been misinformed.

DISCOVERING PURPOSE, CALLING AND GIFTS

The slogan of our ministry is to help people discover and fulfill their purpose. Since I discovered my purpose, I have become passionate about helping people discover theirs. Why? Because I know that once they discover their purpose, their life will have meaning and fulfillment, and they will bear fruit. I have preached and written about this subject in almost all of my books.

In many countries, people think poverty is the problem. Poverty is not the problem; purposelessness is the root of all social ill. I dreamed of coming up with a formula to help humanity discover their purpose. I planned to develop software that would help each individual find their purpose based on their passion and gifts and then start Purpose Revolution Centers in every city.

Then one day, everything changed. Holy Spirit gave me the revelation to crack the purpose code. It was so simple. Though I knew it almost all of my life, I did not recognize it as the purpose of mankind. In this book, I will reveal that secret code, and it will unlock your purpose. Once you finish reading this book, you will never again question the reason for your existence.

God Almighty, Creator of mankind, has made it easy to find our purpose. He knew that without one, we would not accomplish His will on the earth. The sad thing is that even though He made it very easy, most have missed it. As the Word says, He made all things beautiful—but we continually mess things up and come up with many schemes that do not line up with His plans.

Can you imagine that a God like ours would create us and then not tell us why He made us? Would He leave us stranded to waste the majority of our days trying to figure out our purpose? Would He allow a scenario in which we finally figure it out, but then it is too late to do anything about it? He would never do that. After you read this book, you will be sure as the ground you stand on and the air you breathe about why God created mankind in the first place. God made it clear and simple, but man made it complicated, and the religious spirit took advantage of it and confused us to make us ineffective.

The religious spirit, like an epidemic, has killed more people than any dictators, wars, or diseases combined. It has stolen more destinies and potentials than any known disease. For that reason, God's plan and purpose for this planet has been delayed and deviated multiple times. God's intention for helping me write this book is to terminate that epidemic once and for all.

There are three fundamental questions every human asks and for which they need answers. Until they find the answers to those questions, they are not ready to live. Throughout the ages, every wise man has tried to come up with answers to these questions.

These questions are: Who am I? Where did I come from? Why am I here? The first question has to do with *Identity*; the second question has to do with the *Source*; and the third has to do with *Purpose*. Every problem we face is rooted in one of those questions and shows itself in confusion about those answers. That means that the solution to every problem lies in how we answer these questions. If we do not find the right answers, life will not work as it should.

The moment a person is ready to answer those three age-old questions with conviction and clarity, they are ready to live for the first time. Until then, they are living someone else's life or their definition of life. God, in His infinite wisdom, answered all of those questions in Genesis 1, the first chapter of the Bible. He knew that it was critical for mankind and for their function on earth. Unfortunately, we missed it.

God not only wants you to be alive, He wants you to live fully for His glory. He doesn't want you to just survive this life and make it to the other shore, but live a fulfilled life and be able to say at the end of it, "I finished my race." In this book, you will find the answers to those questions as well. I hope you are as excited to read this as I was to write it. This will be the best investment you can make for yourself and the generations to come after you. I pray that God will use this to open your eyes to see life from His perspective and understand His purpose for your life and for our planet Earth. Welcome to the journey.

Abraham John

INTRODUCTION

Jesus said we are the light of this world. Then why does the world seem full of darkness? We have more believers alive today than in all other times combined. The Bible says we are the head and not the tail. Then why do most believers live mediocre lives and in survival mode financially? Jesus said, "I will build my church and the gates of hell shall not prevail against it." Then why were all the first-century churches overthrown by the gates of hell? Though we have hundreds of churches in a city, why do most of our cities remain overtaken by the powers of darkness?

We have more preachers, apostles, churches, believers, and miracle workers in the church today, but more than half the world remains unreached. More believers are dying because of sickness. Why? Something went drastically wrong in the church after the death of the early apostles.

This world is perishing—but not because we do not have enough believers or churches. In fact, we have more of them than at any other time in history. It is perishing because we do not have enough sons and daughters of God on earth who understand the purpose, position, and power given to them by their Father.

We lost our nation, more than half of our families, school systems, media, and everything else we can name, and we blame the devil and everything else for it. However, the real reason we lost all those things is because we walked away from our God-given assignment, and the wicked took that opportunity and filled the vacuum created by our absence. When the light is absent, darkness rules. It is that simple.

In the Bible, nobody preached the heaven and hell message and gave an altar call for those who want to go to heaven. Jesus and the apostles never asked anyone if they wanted to go to heaven or hell when they died. There is a great difference between the people described in the Bible and the believers that are alive today. The people in the Bible knew their purpose very well. *Their goal was not just to make it to heaven, but to make a difference on earth before they died.*

The majority of the people God used in the Bible were Jewish because they were His chosen people. Though they were His chosen people, you didn't see them running around conducting worship concerts and music nights. They knew very well why God created them and chose them. They were focused on that mandate. You will find them on the top of every arena of life in almost every culture.

The early apostles had a different message than what most of church world preaches today. They preached the gospel of the kingdom. *As long as the church preached and practiced the gospel of the kingdom, it remained undefeated.* The moment it deviated and began to preach a religious gospel about taking people to heaven, it lost its power and influence. These days most people preach the gospel of going to heaven.

We have been brainwashed by the religious spirit for so long we don't even recognize it. If you tell a lie enough times, eventually people will believe it as truth. Then when someone discovers the truth and tries to tell us, we will fight with them, thinking it's a lie. That is what is happening to us right now.

God gave us the Holy Spirit and power, so why isn't that power manifesting as it did in the early church? There are two reasons. One is that people have become attached to personalities and particular preachers. If God manifests His power through that preacher, he or she will enlarge their particular ministry, and their bank account becomes bigger. That is almost no benefit to the kingdom of God. Nations and communities will keep going from bad to worse.

He is winding up those kinds of ministers and ministries and raising up a new breed of sons and daughters who are kingdom-minded and who are searching for answers to the solutions their nation and communities are facing. They are not satisfied with the status quo.

The second reason the power of God is not manifesting as it should, though people cry out for it, is that the power of God was released for the purpose of establishing God's kingdom on earth, not to take people from here to heaven. Holy Spirit came as the Governor of the kingdom to help us administer it. If we do not have a grasp of the kingdom and how it works, God will not release His power because people will abuse it for their personal or religious agenda rather than the kingdom agenda.

Before we delve into discovering our purpose, we need to understand some basic principles about the most fundamental beliefs we have in our lives: salvation, worship, purpose, and other beliefs. They are our foundation, and if the foundation is not laid correctly, then nothing else will work correctly either. Fixing this will clear up the misunderstanding we have been believing for a few centuries now, and as a result, it will change everything else around us.

Our nation is in chaos, and we are going toward an implosion. Most Christians have the same old answer: Revival is coming, or the rapture is around the corner.

As the Bible says, "If the *foundations* are destroyed, what can the righteous do?" *(Psalm 11:3)*. It is time to rebuild the foundations. The

DISCOVERING PURPOSE, CALLING AND GIFTS

reason the righteous are feeling helpless is because their foundations have been destroyed. Note the word *foundations* above; this refers to the destruction of the foundations of purpose, family, faith, church, and every other aspect of society.

Finding a job, or a better job is not the solution to financial freedom or creating wealth and riches. Many of us have been programmed to believe that a job is the solution to gaining money. A job is the solution for survival. The kingdom economy doesn't work that way. In the kingdom, discovering your purpose and then gaining specialized knowledge and developing a skill, or using a gift, are the keys to unlocking God's kingdom economy in your life. In fact, I have just released a new book called *Kingdom Economy* that explains how this works in detail.

The first step for your life is to rediscover your purpose, then recognize your calling, identify your gifts, and master them. Purpose is the big *why*, calling is the *what,* and your gifting shows you *how* to do it. Why do we need to rediscover our purpose? We knew it once, but we lost it. Therefore, we need to rediscover it.

After you rediscover your purpose, you need to find your calling. Calling is the area or the aspect of life in which you are specifically called to fulfill that purpose, whether in ministry, business, politics, or any other area. In order to fulfill your calling, you need to identify your gift or develop the necessary skills. Your gifting is the manner in which you fulfill your calling, and eventually your purpose.

May the Lord use this book to bless you and the generations to come to rebuild the foundations the enemy has destroyed. I encourage you to read it more than once and study it and the scriptures mentioned in it. I promise you your life will never be the same. God bless you.

CHAPTER 1
THREE BIGGEST LIES I WAS TAUGHT

Nearly every institution in every nation is going through some form of crisis. When the systems of this world are failing, the sons of God should rise up with the solutions to those crises.

We are the light of *this* world, and light is the solution for darkness, but we have been brainwashed and deceived for a long time by the lies of the enemy. We have been taught to sing that "this world is not my home" and, "Oh, take the whole world, but give me Jesus," and "I'll fly away, oh, glory," "When we all get to heaven," and so on.

These are songs people wrote because of their religious zeal and from a mindset that believed God created man to populate heaven. In other words, God has a shortage of people in heaven so He created earth to function as a "breeding ground." That is absolute blasphemy.

There is a massive deception by the religious spirit among most Christians. They are deceived and lied to about their purpose, their present life, and their future. Those lies have stolen the purposes of millions (maybe billions) of people. Religion and the religious spirit have killed and stolen the potential and dreams of more people than any other demonic spirit.

DISCOVERING PURPOSE, CALLING AND GIFTS

The first lie I was taught as a Christian was that God created man to worship Him, and that worship meant singing. The result of this was that we stayed inside the four walls of a building and sang for hours and hours, thinking we were doing God some kind of favor. After all the singing, I did not see God coming down to deliver us from our miseries. While we were enjoying our musical productions, the enemy came in and stole our government and educational systems.

Actually, we were singing the world to hell! When I got tired of the "worship," the Holy Spirit prompted me to open my Bible and read Genesis to see why God created Adam and what He told him to do with his life. To my surprise, I did not find anything about worship. Another shocking thing I found out is that the word *worship* appears 198 times in the New King James Version of the Bible, and not even once is it mentioned in connection with singing. I said, "What?!"

I believe the first lie came into existence because of David and all the psalms he wrote. After reading those psalms, people came up with their own definition of life, thinking God might have created them to sing to Him, without understanding the lives of those people who actually wrote the ancient psalms.

Those writing the new songs did not understand what those people had done with their lives. David was the greatest king of Israel and Moses was a deliverer. Singing was not their purpose; reigning in life was their focus. We were taught that if we just sing and dance like David, we will become another David, and one day God will bless us.

The second lie I was taught was that we are pilgrims and strangers on this earth, so we should not get involved in politics or business because the earth and its resources belong to the devil and his children. This lie comes from a faulty perception of what is written in Hebrews where it says the Old Testament believers were pilgrims and strangers on earth.

They quoted Hebrews 11:13–16, without understanding that the author was simply saying that the Old Testament saints could not receive the promises God gave them because they did not have the privilege of hearing the message of the kingdom. Those viewing the church in this light tend to forget that almost everyone God used in the Bible (even Jesus and Paul) was involved in, or connected to, the government (politics) of their time in some way or form. Even prophets like Elijah and Elisha were connected to the government of their time *(1 Kings 17:1; 2 Kings 4:13)*.

I will explain why they were strangers and pilgrims. Many use the verse from Hebrews 11 as an excuse to remain poor or for their lack of productivity. They think this present life on earth is not important, and the one to come is the most important. Until they recognize what they have now, and realize that they are responsible to use it for God's kingdom here on earth, they will keep going on like this. Scripture actually teaches that each of us will receive a reward according to our works and investment we make into the kingdom in this life *(1 Corinthians 3:8)*.

Most of the Old Testament saints were billionaires, if we calculate their wealth in today's value. They established and conquered nations, owned vast amounts of land and agriculture, cattle and servants. They were not poor in any way or form. They were the richest people of their times. This includes people like Abraham, Noah, Adam, David, Solomon, Job, and Boaz, just to name a few.

The reason the Bible says they were pilgrims and strangers is this: Since Adam lost Eden and the kingdom, all the saints since then were looking forward to a country whose maker and builder was God. God promised them restoration and rest, but they could not enter the rest because Jesus hadn't died yet. The sin of the world was not remitted, so they all died only seeing those promises by faith, but never obtaining them.

> These all died in faith, not having received the prom- ises, but having seen them afar off, were assured of them, embraced them and confessed that they were strangers and pilgrims on the earth. For those who say such things declare plainly that they seek a homeland. And truly if they had called to mind that country from which they had come out, they would have had opportunity to return. But now they desire a better, that is, a heavenly country. Therefore God is not ashamed to be called their God, for He has prepared a city for them. (Hebrews 11:13-16)

Note that the first verse says they all died in faith not having received the promises. Which promises is the author talking about? The promise of the Messiah and the kingdom He was going to bring.

> And all these, having obtained a good testimony through faith, did not receive the promise, God having provided something better for us, that they should not be made perfect apart from us. (Hebrews 11:39-40)

Then again, Hebrews goes on to say, "Therefore, since we are receiving a kingdom which cannot be shaken, let us have grace, by which we may serve God acceptably with reverence and godly fear" *(Hebrews 12:28).*

The Bible never says the Old Testament believers received the kingdom that we received. Jesus, when He revealed the mysteries of the kingdom in Matthew, said: "For assuredly, I say to you that many prophets and righteous men desired to see what you see, and did not see it, and to hear what you hear, and did not hear it" (Matthew 13:17).

Jesus was talking about the kingdom and its works that He came to reveal. None of the generations in the Old Testament had the privilege of seeing and living in that kingdom. Some of them saw it by faith, but it was in a different time frame.

THREE BIGGEST LIES I WAS TAUGHT

The third lie I was taught was that I will go to heaven and worship or sing hallelujah for thousands of years. Well, that is not in the Bible either. The Bible says the same thing about our purpose in its first and the last chapters—Genesis 1 and Revelation 22. God never changed His mind concerning us, or asked us to take a break from our purpose in this life. He will never do that.

If you have been deceived by the enemy, it is time to shake off those deceptions and rise up from the ashes. This world needs us now more than ever. I read statistics recently that said 70% of our youth walk away from their faith once they leave their homes or after college. Whose fault is this? We have not done a good job preparing them to influence this world for Christ. We did not teach them about their purpose. Let's preach the truth without any compromise or apology. Don't let the fear of man or the religious spirit rob you of your destiny. May the Lord help us do this!

Before you read further, please make sure you are free from these three lies and their strongholds are broken off of your mind. Otherwise, you will not benefit much from the rest of this book.

CHAPTER 2
UNDERSTANDING SALVATION

The Bible says in all our getting, to get understanding *(Proverbs 4:7)*. There is only one reason we perish and that is because of a lack of knowledge *(Hosea 4:6)*. *Ignorance is deadly.* If a person is ignorant and doesn't recognize it, that is even more deadly. Let's go over some of the foundational doctrines of our faith.

If we do not understand and lay our foundation correctly, we cannot build anything on it that will stand. The reason believers remain ineffective in most places is because they have been misinformed about their purpose. We inherited a gloom and despair eschatology. We have been living on a shaky and unsure foundation.

Another sad scenario with the majority of the believers is that they do not understand what salvation is all about. The doctrine of salvation is the most misunderstood doctrine in the Bible, next to purpose. We believe salvation is all about making it to heaven when we die or when Jesus comes. Most are taught that we lost heaven when Adam fell. They received a religious concept that said God created man to live in heaven or we fell from heaven, and we lost it and for some reason, we are stuck on earth now (did God make a mistake?), and God sent Jesus to take us all back to heaven.

Jesus talked about the born-again experience only once to a Jewish religious leader in a private meeting during the middle of the night. He never preached it in public or told any Gentile about being born-again. That really shocked me. Think about it and research it in the Bible.

Why and how did this salvation program of God come about? The whole program came because of the fall of Adam, right? Everyone universally accepts that fact. But some have forgotten from where Adam fell, and what he lost because of the fall. Through salvation, God's intent was to restore man to the position and place Adam was before the fall. If that is not your understanding of salvation, then you were influenced by the religious spirit somewhere along the way.

Where did Adam fall from? What did he lose because of the fall? What kind of relationship did he have with God before the fall, and what was he required to do before he met with God every day? What would Adam and his children be doing now if he hadn't fallen? The

Bible does not mention any particular requirement Adam was required to perform, other than show up when God came down and called him. They had a father/son relationship. The Bible says Adam was the son of God *(Luke 3:38)*.

Adam did not have to sing three fast songs and then two slow songs before he met with God or to feel His presence in the garden. Eden and heaven were united in every aspect. When we are saved, the first thing God does for us is to restore our position as His children. *We became part of His family.*

> But as many as received Him, to them He gave the right to become children of God, to those who believe in His name. (John 1:12)

After we become God's children, we are supposed relate to Him as our Father, just like Adam and Jesus did. All the singing and worship came because of the fall. I have explained this in detail in another book. We are supposed to go to Him as a child goes to His Father and talk and commune with Him anytime we choose. After we are saved, everything we do in life has to flow from that foundation of our relationship with God as our Father. If not, things will not work the way they should. That is why most Christians are struggling in their life. *They are waiting to escape from the assignment God gave them.*

Where Adam failed, God gave us another example to show how a son or daughter is supposed to connect with their heavenly Father. That is none other than Jesus, the Son of the Living God. The Bible calls Jesus the last Adam. How did Jesus connect with His Father while He was here on earth? Or how did the disciples connect with Jesus? They were not required to sing four songs each morning before they came into His presence. He was with them all the time. He is with us all the time now.

Our theology has been twisted and manipulated by ignorance and by the religious spirit. Because we have been doing some things for so long, we think that it is normal or that it is the way it always has been or should be. It was not like this for all of time. And we teach others the things we "know" with great passion. It is not helping them nor is it helping us. We have been hiding behind a religious mask. We know in our hearts something has been missing or out of place all along.

We do need to praise and magnify God. When we do it, we have to do the best we can and give Him the maximum glory that is due His name. We need to do it for the right reasons too. In the New Testament, we praise Him for what He does. In Acts 2 we read that they praised God—not to feel His presence, but as an act of gratitude.

> So continuing daily with one accord in the temple, and breaking bread from house to house, they ate their food

DISCOVERING PURPOSE, CALLING AND GIFTS

with gladness and simplicity of heart, praising God and having favor with all the people. And the Lord added to the church daily those who were being saved. (Acts 2:46-47)

In another place in Acts 3, we read of the lame man who was healed. He walked, leaped and praised God for the miracle. He was thanking and praising God for healing him. That is what we should be doing. When God does an amazing act, we should all come together to praise and thank Him. We should not do this as some sort of religious duty every time we meet so we can feel the presence of God. Either God is in you or you are not saved. It's that simple.

When you are born again, Jesus comes to dwell within you. You become the temple of God and of His Holy Spirit. *You become His residence.* If He is in you and you are not feeling Him, then there is something blocking that feeling. You need to find out what it is and why. I used to be all about praise and worship music. Because I was raised in the religious circle, I did what I was taught. I did not understand the truth. I bought all types of cassette tapes and CDs of praise and worship music. I played them and felt good; I had my favorites that gave me special emotional goosebumps. Then I received the revelation of sonship and the New Testament teaching on the temple of God and threw them away. My focus changed completely.

I had a rough childhood, and my relationship with my father was not healthy. I had a hard time relating to my heavenly Father, too, because our concept of a father is formed by our relationship with our earthly father. I had to go through a healing process to understand God's love for me. When I did that, I began to relate to God as my Father on a moment-by-moment basis like Adam and Jesus did, not on a weekend basis or when I heard a particular type of music. Now I sense Him all the time. He is faithful to show me if there is anything in my life that is not pleasing to Him.

UNDERSTANDING SALVATION

If you do not feel or sense God's (Holy Spirit) presence on a continual basis, there is something blocking it. You need to find out what that is and deal with it. It is not God's problem that you are not feeling Him; it is the blockage or wound in your soul that needs to be dealt with.

> But he who is joined to the Lord is one spirit with Him. (1 Corinthians 6:17)

You have been made one with Him. There is no separation between you and God. If you feel a separation, then it is on your side that the problem exists.

> The Spirit of truth, whom the world cannot receive, because it neither sees Him nor knows Him; but you know Him, for He dwells with you and will be in you. (John 14:17)

> Jesus answered and said to him, "If anyone loves Me, he will keep My word; and My Father will love him, and We will come to him and make Our home with him". (John 14:23)

Everything on earth and in heaven has been reconciled and brought together in Christ Jesus as it was in Eden. There is no broken relationship between heaven and earth, or man and God. Everything has been reconciled in Christ Jesus and brought to peace. Do you see it manifest in the natural? No. Because not very many people believe it and play their part to restore it. They keep cursing the earth and what God has created. They are all waiting to fly away instead!

> That in the dispensation of the fullness of the times He might gather together in one all things in Christ, both which are in heaven and which are on earth—in Him. (Ephesians 1:10)

> For it pleased the Father that in Him all the fullness should dwell, and by Him to reconcile all things to Himself, by Him, whether things on earth or things in heaven, having made peace through the blood of His cross. (Colossians 1:19-20)

God is raising up a new generation of sons and daughters who will fully understand and walk in the revelation Adam had in God before the fall. I dedicate this book to that group of people. This book is not about rapture and revival. If you are looking for that, then you are wasting your time. This book is intended to restore the foundation that has been broken down for generations.

When you read it, some things might sound strange or shocking. But if there is a Holy Spirit in you, He will bear witness with your spirit that this is the word of the Lord for you right now. God talks about that generation of people in Isaiah:

> Thus says the Lord: "In an acceptable time I have heard You, and in the day of salvation I have helped You; I will preserve You and give You as a covenant to the people, to restore the earth, to cause them to inherit the desolate heritages". (Isaiah 49:8)

> Those from among you shall build the old waste places; you shall raise up the foundations of many generations; and you shall be called the Repairer of the Breach, the Restorer of Streets to Dwell In. (Isaiah 58:12)

> And they shall rebuild the old ruins, they shall raise up the former desolations, and they shall repair the ruined cities, the desolations of many generations. (Isaiah 61:4)

If the earth is waiting to be burned or destroyed, when do you think those above verses will be fulfilled? I believe it is happening now.

UNDERSTANDING SALVATION

If those verses were only meant for the people of Israel and their land, then they would not speak about restoring the whole earth. This book is to equip the body of Christ to become part of that restoration process.

If you are saved, you need to return from where you have fallen. If you are to be restored, you need to know what you lost. I remember hearing the story of a drunkard. One night he was coming home, and when he reached his house he couldn't find his keys. He retraced his steps, looking for a streetlight. When he found one, he began to search for his keys under that light. He kept looking and looking for hours and could not find the keys.

One of his friends came by and asked him what he was searching for. He told him he had lost his keys and was looking for them. His friend asked if he knew where he lost them, and the drunkard replied that he didn't know, but he saw the light and thought he would find them there if he looked.

That story is similar to many people's lives. We don't know what we have lost or where to find it, but have been searching and searching all of our lives in the light we have found. I pray that God will use this book to end that search. If you need to know what we lost when Adam fell and how God restored everything to us through Jesus Christ, please read my book **Discovering the Lost Kingdom.**

CHAPTER 3
UNDERSTANDING WORSHIP

As I mentioned earlier, one of the lies the devil uses to deceive countless numbers of believers worldwide is that God created man to worship Him. To most, worship means singing. What did God tell Adam about worship? If that was the purpose, did God forget to mention it to Adam? How did Adam relate with God in the garden? What are the rituals and ceremonies he had to perform in order to please God? How many songs did he sing before God showed up in the garden every day?

As I mentioned earlier, Adam had a father/son relationship with God. The Bible says Adam was the son of God *(Luke 3:38)*. In the natural, what is a son required to do before he can meet with his father? Normally nothing. He has the right to meet with his father anytime, unless his father is in some form of closed meeting or in prison. In normal circumstances, a father and son can meet anytime, anywhere. That was the case in Eden. God came down every day to meet with Adam, not just on Sunday morning. They walked and talked as long as they chose.

That is the kind of relationship God wants with us, too. We are His children. Once you believe in Jesus Christ, you become a child of God, and He becomes your Father from that moment on. How much you want to grow in that relationship is up to you. Unfortunately, many precious saints never grow in their relationship with Him. Their relationship remains rigidly steeped in Old Testament theology. They think they have to sing three or four songs before God will show up. They are not trained to recognize and release the God who dwells in them.

Don't misunderstand me; we all begin there. When we were babies, we did not have much understanding about who our natural father was, what kind of person he was, his nature and character. As we grew up, our understanding also increased. When we are mature, we have a different level of relationship with him than when we were babies. The same thing should happen in our relationship with our heavenly Father.

Jesus promised that where two or three are gathered in His name anywhere, He will be there in the midst of them *(Matthew 18:20)*. He did not say He will only come if we sing three songs first. Playing music didn't start almost a thousand years after Adam was created. It was Cain's grandson who was the father of all music we hear today *(Genesis 4:21)*.

Why was there so much singing and music in the Old Testament after the fall? God created humans to be a dwelling place or a temple for Him. After the fall of man, God could not dwell in humans. So He dwelt in two places; one was in the Holy of Holies in the tabernacle or in the temple, and the other was in the praises of His people. So David appointed singers and musicians to sing and praise God twenty-four hours a day in the tent he pitched. *David knew he could create a temporary dwelling place for God through music and he wanted God's presence around him all the time.* That is the way it began.

Once we are born again, we are supposed to have a Father/child relationship with God. Many live in fear and dread of God; thinking if they do not sing to God, He might punish them with some sickness or accident. Our God is not like that. He is merciful and kind.

How did Jesus relate with His Father while He was on earth? How many songs did He have to sing before He could talk with His Father? He talked with Him anytime He chose. The same was true of the disciples and Jesus. The Bible says Jesus is our older Brother. We are born into the same family. He is the Firstborn from the dead *(Colossians 1:18)*. We are bone of His bones and flesh of His flesh *(Ephesians 5:30)*.

If your relationship with God is a Master/slave or Creator/creature relationship, you will have difficulty understanding this. Many people have trouble relating to God as their Father because they did not have a father who was a positive role model. Many were abused by their fathers—physically, emotionally and sexually. If you are one of them, then you will definitely be challenged in this area. You may need to find some professional help to get healed from that father-wound.

I recently met a woman who has been in ministry for several decades. She told me that she will never call God her Father. She said she only talks to Jesus. It is because of the abusive background she grew up in with her earthly father. She hasn't found the healing for it yet.

Even Satan understood what worship meant when he asked Jesus to fall down and worship him. He did not ask Jesus to stand and sing four songs or even fall down and sing. According to the Bible, falling at someone's feet is real worship *(Matthew 2:11, 4:8–9; Revelation 5:14; 22:8)*.

WHAT IS TRUE WORSHIP?

Worship is not what we say with our mouths. Many people believe that if they go to a building called a church and sing three songs, they worshipped God. According to the Bible, they did not worship God at all.

> Therefore, the Lord said: "Inasmuch as these people draw near with their mouths and honor Me with their lips, but

have removed their hearts far from Me, and their fear toward
Me is taught by the commandment of men". (Isaiah 29:13)

When we leave the place we call church, what we do with our life is the real worship. Many go and do their own thing. Some go to a movie theater to watch a movie after church on Sunday. Some run to their favorite sports game or to a shopping mall. How did their worship help God, the earth, or their own lives? Jesus addresses this in Matthew, in the New Testament.

These people draw near to Me with their mouth, and honor Me with their lips, but their heart is far from Me. *And in vain they worship Me*, teaching as doctrines the commandments of men. (Matthew 15:8-9)

We think it's our life and we can do whatever we want with it, but your life does not belong to you. It belongs to God. We were sold as slaves to sin, and Jesus bought us with a price because of His love *(1 Corinthians 6:20)*. Once we were purchased, we belong to Him from that moment onwards. We are supposed to use our lives to do His will.

We compartmentalize our lives. We tell God that He can have access to these particular areas but that we are in charge and decide what we do with the rest. We keep God out of many areas of our lives. *That means we have not accepted Jesus Christ as our Lord in those areas yet.*

There is a world of difference between accepting Jesus as our Savior and accepting Him as our Lord. Most people accept Him as their Savior to go to heaven but not as their Lord to live on earth. We may have mumbled something with our mouth, but we did not mean it in our hearts. Everything belongs to God—every moment we are alive and the very air we breathe.

Many people are confused about praise and worship. They misunderstand praise for worship. They are as different as night and day.

UNDERSTANDING WORSHIP

What is real worship? The answer to that question will vary from person to person. To Abel, it was to bring the firstborn of his flock.

> Abel also brought of the firstborn of his flock and of their fat. And the Lord respected Abel and his offering. (Genesis 4:4)

To Abraham, it was extreme obedience: When Abraham took his son Isaac to sacrifice, "Abraham told his servants, 'Stay here with the donkey; the lad and I will go yonder and worship, and we will come back to you'" *(Genesis 22:5)*.

To Joshua, it was to fall on his face: "And Joshua fell on his face to the earth and worshiped, and said to Him, 'What does my Lord say to His servant?'" *(Joshua 5:14)*.

To David, it was to dwell in the house of the Lord to behold His beauty. David wrote: "One thing I have desired of the Lord, that will I seek: that I may dwell in the house of the Lord all the days of my life, to behold the beauty of the Lord, and to inquire in His temple" *(Psalm 27:4)*.

To the wise men from the east, falling down before Jesus and presenting Him with the gifts they brought was worship.

> "And when they had come into the house, they saw the young Child with Mary His mother, and fell down and worshiped Him. And when they had opened their treasures, they presented gifts to Him: gold, frankincense, and myrrh.". (Matthew 2:2, 11)

To Jesus, it was to worship the Father in spirit and in truth, not with singing and dancing.

> But the hour is coming, and now is, when the true worshippers will worship the Father in spirit and truth; for the

DISCOVERING PURPOSE, CALLING AND GIFTS

Father is seeking such to worship Him. God is Spirit, and those who worship Him must worship in spirit and truth. (John 4:23- 24)

Those are just a few examples of what true worship means in the Bible.

We have been programmed about singing for generations. It became the main focus of our Christian life and we began calling it *worship*. That was not the case in the lives of the people in the Bible. How many songs did Adam, Abel, Noah, Abraham, Moses, Joseph, Joshua, Esther, Paul and Jesus sing in their lifetimes? I do not know, but they were not confused between singing a song and their worship of God.

We see Moses sang at least two times, and Jesus and the disciples sang a hymn and Paul praised God while he was in the Philippian jail. Paul also wrote that he sang with the spirit *(Acts 16:25; 1 Corinthians 14:15)*. So they all sang to some degree, *but they worshiped God with their lives on a daily basis.* They lived to the fullest and brought maximum glory to the name of God.

I am not against singing, but I am against suggesting that the act of singing fulfills our purpose. Robbing people of their potential and destinies for the sake of religion is a crime against humanity. I am not against any form of worship. I have been worshiping God with my life, and I will do it until my last breath. However, many have misunderstood what true worship is and how to do it. How did people in the Bible's days worship God? What is true worship? When did it begin and who does it benefit most?

We need to lay aside our ideas about singing first because worship is not singing. We have been taught and practiced that idea, but it is in error. So let's think outside of that box. The word *worship* appears the first time in Genesis 22 where Abraham went to offer Isaac as a sacrifice. He went to the foot of the mountain and asked his servants to stay there while he and Isaac went and worshiped and came back.

UNDERSTANDING WORSHIP

What did Abraham and Isaac do on the top of the mountain? How did they worship God there? To Abraham, extreme obedience was worship. He was honoring God with all His life. Abraham did not give lip service, saying "I surrender all" to God on that mountain. He did not have a concert on top of that mountain either. Abraham's worship cost him almost everything he had.

Today people live all types of immoral lives and come to church on Sunday to sing and jump and think they are worshiping God. That is not accurate.

To me, worship is honoring God. Singing is the least and the easiest way we can honor Him. God is not that impressed with our mere words. He said His people honored Him with their words, but their hearts were not with Him. He was not pleased with that in Old Testament times.

He was not pleased with that when Jesus walked the earth, and He is not pleased with that now. In fact, He is disgusted by it.

When we maximize the opportunities, potential, and resources God gave us, and are faithful stewards of the earth He gave us, we worship Him. In other words, fulfilling our God-given purpose is the greatest form of worship we can give to God. How can someone fulfill their purpose if they do not know what that is? That's why God gave you this book. We haven't maximized anything yet on this earth. Believers are some of the least productive people on the entire planet. They are all waiting for a miracle from God to reach the next level, while an unbeliever will work hard and use everything they have.

I am all for true worship, but we need to understand what it is and follow God according to His Word. Too many sing to God because of fear of punishment, thinking this is their worship. Deep down in their hearts, they believe that if they do not sing to God, they are disobedient and will suffer some misfortune. We need a revelation of God as our Father. Though we call Him Father, in practice, we have a creature and Creator relationship or a Master and slave relationship. We are afraid God will harm us and are afraid. That fear is not of Him; that fear comes from the religious spirit.

I lived with that fear for a long time. I did not know how to relate to God as my Father. Because of my poor experience with my earthly father, I had father wounds, which distorted my view of God and allowed me to harbor irrational fears about Him. Most of the time I felt like the Israelites at the foot of Mount Sinai when God appeared on the top. They saw the fire and heard the thunder, and they were scared. They cried out to Moses, begging him not to let them see such things again. They wanted him to go to the top to see and receive the message from God instead.

Below are some common misunderstandings about worship:

"WORSHIP" EQUALS PRAISE, WHICH HAS BEEN TAUGHT AS OUR PURPOSE

It is generally taught that worship and singing are the same thing, so for most people, worship means singing. Maybe in their heart they believe differently, but when it comes to their actions, they believe that if they are not singing, then they are not worshiping God. That is not true. In the Bible, the majority of the time the word *worship* appears, it means to fall down at someone's feet or bow down before someone.

God did not create man to "worship" Him in praise. We do praise Him because we love Him, but that is only one of the ways we express our love toward Him. As we will explore in greater depth in the coming pages, our complete worship refers to *everything* in our life that honors God. This includes obedience to His mandate for our lives.

PRAISE PRACTICED OUT OF FEAR

As I mentioned earlier, many sing because of fear. We need to sing from a heart of gratitude and not of fear. Praise is simply the overflow of our hearts for all that He has done for us.

TO PLEASE GOD

Many believe that if they sing to God, He will be pleased with them and bless them, without knowing God is already pleased with them. Jesus came to announce the acceptable year of the Lord. That does not mean just any year, but as long as this age remains, God is pleased with us *(Luke 4:19)*. Not based on our works, but on what Jesus did on the cross.

IT'S A STAGE WE NEED TO GO THROUGH

We all begin our life living in and under the law, and then mature into the Word of righteousness and grace to experience freedom in Christ. Unfortunately, many do not ever cross over to that freedom; they live under the law and die under the curse of it.

We all need to go through the stage of sensing God's presence through singing or other external stimuli. I remember days when I would hear a particular song and immediately sense God through my emotions. I would become "addicted" to that song for a while and eventually I would "grow" out of it. Then a new song or music would come and take the place of the old one. I went through that cycle for over twenty years.

I started two "worship" teams that led songs or played the keyboard for me before and while I preached. I wasn't sure God was with me or in me. I had to overcome terrible insecurities when it came to my relation- ship with Him and my calling. *I thought He was with me only when*

I felt Him. To be honest, I was afraid of losing Him or Him leaving my life, especially if I did something that was not pleasing to Him.

The enemy used fear to torment me, causing me to feel that I had lost my anointing or that God had rejected me and would not use me again. Again, I would wait until I could feel Him to make sure He hadn't left me and did not take His anointing away from me.

Sometimes days and weeks went by in which I did not feel Him. I did not feel that stirring or goose bumps in my spirit, and I used to get really depressed and tormented by doubts. Thank God He did not leave me there, and I did not stay in that stage forever. I did not know how to connect with Him as my Father moment by moment. I was living based on my feelings. The Bible called me a carnal believer *(1 Corinthians 3:3)*. That is what the Bible calls those who are led by their feelings and emotions.

I did not know how to live by faith. The Bible commands us to walk by faith, not by feeling or sight *(2 Corinthians 5:7)*. I did not know how to believe what the Word said and live by it. I only knew how to connect with God in the realm of my feelings. If I felt Him in my spirit, then I believed He was there, and if I did not feel, then I thought He wasn't.

I read in the Bible that whatever did not originate in faith was sin *(Romans 14:23),* but I did not realize I was sinning every time I tried to feel God by doing something, instead of believing what the Word said and living by faith. In truth, I was trying to manipulate God to do something to satisfy my carnality and my insecurity.

I was a baby Christian. When I was a baby in the natural, I always wanted to feel my mother or have her next to me. When I woke up from sleep and couldn't see her, I cried for her attention. If I couldn't feel her, then I thought she wasn't there. When I became an adult, I did not do that anymore. I knew my mother was there. When I moved to another country and left my parents, I didn't cry every day for their attention. I just knew by faith they were there and safe.

Too many believers are still at this infant level in their relationship with God. They have parked their life around an experience they had with God many years ago when they started their walk with the Lord. They have become traditional, but they think they are led by the Spirit and free in Christ. Once you depend on a tradition (even if it is without your knowledge), the religious spirit takes over your life.

Once in a while, this religious spirit will cause you to feel an emotional high and you will think it is the Holy Spirit. You will think you had a great day or experience with God based on what you felt. However, if you check your life afterward and nothing major has changed, then you are still at the same level as before.

Year after year, even decades, can go by like this. In reality, this person is not any better than a religious monk who lives in the mountains of Tibet and wakes up every morning and repeats the same mantra he has been repeating for the last forty years. He believes by doing that, that he is doing some favor to his deity and "one day" something extraordinary is going to happen, and he is going to attain eternal bliss.

Unfortunately, hundreds or maybe thousands of monks have died without ever achieving that eternal bliss or enlightenment. Because of his belief and fear of losing something, mixed with his religiosity, he is afraid to stop or try anything new. Every year, millions of people die as victims of the religious spirit. We have been doing the same thing for generations, and many have died without ever achieving or fulfilling their purpose.

DISCOVERING PURPOSE, CALLING AND GIFTS

I thank my God for not leaving me in that stage for the rest of my life. Through trials and errors, I learned to relate to God as my Father and how to walk by faith by choosing to believe what the Word says, whether I felt anything or not. At first, it was hard, but the longer I lived, the easier it became. My faith muscle grew, and now I can activate and step out in faith to do what the Word says, whether I feel like it or not.

That is why Paul says this:

> Now I say that the heir, as long as he is a child, does not differ at all from a slave, though he is master of all, but is under guardians and stewards until the time appointed by the father. Even so we, when we were children, were in bondage under the elements of the world. But when the fullness of the time had come, God sent forth His Son, born of a woman, born under the law, to redeem those who were under the law, that we might receive the adoption as sons. And because you are sons, God has sent forth the Spirit of His Son into your hearts, crying out, "Abba, Father!" Therefore, you are no longer a slave but a son, and if a son, then an heir of God through Christ. (Galatians 4:1-7)

This says we are the masters of everything God created, as long as we are acting like a son. Unfortunately, most believers today are living in the childish stage. They haven't matured enough to manifest the image and likeness of God to the rest of creation. A mature son or daughter will do what their father does or better than what he does.

TRUE WORSHIP

So what is true worship? Honoring God with your life is worship.

Extreme obedience is worship. Maximizing your potential is worship. Maximizing your opportunities is worship, and maximizing your resources is worship. Falling at His feet is worship, and bowing down is worship.

One day, a dear friend of mine asked me about worship after reading one of our monthly newsletters. It included the section on the three lies I had been taught as a Christian. They were shocked

to read what I wrote about worship. I wrote a reply, and I feel led to insert it here:

> *Hi! Thank you so much for reaching out with your concern. I really appreciate that. I will try my best, with the help of the Holy Spirit, to explain what I can through this message. I hope you understood that the three lies I was taught came from my personal experience. I grew up in church all my life and wherever I went, they taught me that God created mankind to worship Him. I thought man's purpose was to worship, and I was taught that worship mainly meant singing songs. I did that for a very long time. I even started two worship (praise) teams, one from our church in India, and another one with the chil- dren from our vision center there. I believed I had to sing songs before God could manifest or before I could feel His presence. I even had keyboard players wherever I went to preach. I had them play in the background before I preached because I wanted to "feel" the Holy Spirit. I bought all the CDs I could, and I still have many of them.*
>
> *That was a stage I went through in the process of my growth in walking with God. Thank God I did not stop there. The theology I was taught was based on the Old Covenant (Old Testament) after the fall. I grew up in a town in India where there were at least 250 churches (most of them with less than fifty believers), but nothing changed for the better in my home-*

town for hundreds of years. All these churches were "worshiping" God at least three times a week. The gospel came to India with the apostle Thomas. I was disappointed, so I went to God with my problem. He told me to read Genesis 1–2 to see why God created mankind. I did not see God telling Adam and Eve anything about worship or singing. I thought maybe He forgot to tell them. God was very clear about how and why He was creating mankind. Our Creator's purpose statement could be found in Genesis 1:26.

How did Adam and Eve connect with God? What did they have to do before meeting with God on a daily basis? As far as I know, they did not have to do anything. All they had to do was show up. Because they had a Father-child relationship with God Almighty (Luke 3:38), they walked and talked with God every day until sin entered through disobedience.

Sin distorted our view about ourselves and God. **Man lost the ability to relate with God as Father.** *I had a natural father. To talk to him, all I had to do was show up. Any time of the day! After the fall, God couldn't dwell in people because of sin.*

With God's direction, Old Testament saints figured out ways to relate to God. First, He allowed them to create a dwelling place for Him. This was the tabernacle which later became the temple, and the second way was praising. God indwelt the praises of His people (Psalm 22:3). To sum that up, in the Old Covenant, God dwelt in the Holy of Holies and in the praises of His people.

That means that whenever or as long as they sang or played music, God showed up, and the moment they stopped, His presence lifted. All the psalms David wrote were from that perspective. But God never intended to leave us on our own or alone. Because of His mercy and love toward us, He brought a *plan of "salvation" to restore and reinstate what we lost because of the fall. The first thing restored was our **sonship**. Believing in Jesus made us a child of God (John 1:12). That moment when God became my Father was the same as Adam in the garden. That revelation changed everything for me. Now I walk and talk with Him moment by moment. I do not need music or singing to feel Him. He dwells in me.*

The next thing He showed me was how Jesus related to our Father while He was on earth. Did He do something or sing to feel God? He said He and the Father are one. How did the disciples relate to Jesus? In the New Testament, we are told that we are the temple of God, and the Holy Spirit dwells within us (1 Corinthians 3:16 and 6:19).

*If you are a child of God, He dwells in you 24/7. He does not take a break or a vacation. Christ **in you** the hope of glory. If anyone **is in** Christ (2 Corinthians 5:17). By saying that, do we need to sing and praise God? Of course we do. But singing should not be confused with my purpose. Singing is not my purpose. As long as we live, we will praise God. As the Bible says: Everything God created praises Him, but that is not their purpose.*

*A cow was created to give milk; the sun was created to give light. That's their **purpose**. Praising is part of their **function**. If a cow does not give milk, it will end up as hamburgers. If you look in the church world, we are so caught up singing that we are not fulfilling our purpose. It is very sad that most believers are still living based on this Old Covenant theology. They do not know how to relate with God as their Father. **Our purpose is to rule and reign on earth and to establish God's kingdom and will here, as it is in heaven.***

The whole creation is waiting for the manifestation of the sons of God (Romans 8:19-21). This will not happen by singing. That is why we do not see anywhere in the New Testament that a church service should begin with forty minutes or more of singing. If I praise Him but neglect to fulfill my purpose, I will not get any reward when He returns, and He or the earth do not get any benefit from my life.

As I said before, the word "worship" appears 198 times in the entire Bible, and not even once is it mentioned in relation to singing or praising. I did not make this up. Check it out for yourself. When I first read it, it shocked me, and I know this is a touchy subject. We have been programmed for hundreds of years, and it's not easy to change.

If you study the Jewish people of our day, they are the direct descendants of David, yet we do not see very many music teams or praise teams, and Jesus is the Son of David! They do not go from town to town or nation to nation, leading people in song. However, you will see them in every aspect of life in our society: government, media, technology, business, you name it, they will be the most influential people and they will be very involved. Why? Because they understand very well why God created them. They were not taught "Jesus loves me this I know" from their childhood. They were brought up to rule, mandated by God to do that, and they understand it.

*Another thing that surprised me is that the Bible is very clear about our purpose. Genesis 1:26, Revelation 5:9–10, and again, Revelation 22:5, all say we will be ruling and reigning **on earth** forever and ever. I have still not found a single song or hymn in all of Christendom that says we were created to reign (and if you do, please send it to me). But there are hundreds of* *songs that say we will be flying away soon and will be singing praises for thousands of years. The Bible does not say that. I am sorry. This is the best explanation I can give you right now. If you have any further questions or need clarification on anything I have written, please reach out. I will be happy to address them. Thank you very much, and may God bless you.*

CHAPTER 4

UNDERSTANDING PURPOSE

WHAT IS PURPOSE?

How many of you wish you had raised your children a little differently than the way you did? Or wished your parents raised you differently than the way they did? We all have regrets. As parents of three teenagers, though they are wonderful, I already wish I had done some things differently when they were little. In truth, all parents wish they had another chance to raise their children again.

Are there certain things about life that you wish you had known sooner? What if you knew twenty years ago what you know now? After reading one of the books this ministry publishes, many people say they wish they had read that book twenty or forty years ago. So what will we do with our experience? Are we going to hide it because of ego or share it to make a difference for the next generation?

Every father wants his children to grow up and do what he does, but better. That is why we see children following in their father's footsteps and taking over businesses, ministries, churches, politics, trades, and more. Jesus did not come to earth to fulfill His dreams, but to do the will of His Father who sent Him. Then He said we would do greater things than He did. Sometimes with our religiously programmed and limited mindset, we think of it as more or greater miracles.

What greater miracles can we do than Jesus did? Raising the dead, walking on water, and walking through walls? Jesus already did all those with ease. Making the lame walk? He did that more than anyone else did so far. Then what could He have meant by that?

First of all, Jesus did not say "greater miracles"; He said "greater works." There is a big difference between the two. I believe He meant restoring a nation back to God, becoming a prime minister or president of a nation. As God's children, we're supposed to grow up and do what He does in the manner He does it.

Now the question is: What does He do? Again, we think all God does is heal, save and deliver. That is only a fraction of what He does. First of all, He creates because He is the Creator of all. As His children, we need to create things, invent new products and ideas, and develop those inventions. Jesus also redeems, rules, restores, rebuilds, and establishes. We need to train believers and release them into the manufacturing sector of our countries.

Purpose is the reason for which something exists—the original intent for which it is created or made. Only the manufacturer knows the purpose of a product. An apple tree was created with one intention: produce apples. There are many kinds of apples. Mango trees were created with one intention: produce mangoes. There are various kinds of mangoes. If those trees are not producing fruit, they are useless and will be cut down and used for something for which they were not created.

Cows were created to give milk and sun was created to give light and heat. God was very clear about man's purpose when He created him. Do not believe anyone's definition of the purpose of your life. Do not let others define or write the script for your life. God already wrote your script. I am not saying that out of rebellion. In my own experience, people always have an opinion of how you should live your life.

There is only one place we should receive the script and purpose for our lives. That is through God and His Word. The sad thing is that religious spirits have twisted the Word, and made millions of people believe the lies of the devil. They think what they believe is in the Bible, but they never take the time to find out whether or not what they believe is really scriptural and whether it was meant for them.

For a long time, I believed the lie of the devil. I was a Spirit-filled believer, or I thought I was Spirit-filled; later I found out that it was the religious spirit that filled me. The number one sign of the religious spirit operating in your life is that you will not know your purpose. You will be confused about why you exist or the reason you wake up every morning. If I had been filled with the Holy Spirit, I would have been in alignment with God about my purpose and identity.

To understand the purpose of a thing or a product, we need to understand its source. If something came out of something, it carries the same DNA and essence of the source. To understand our purpose, we need to understand our Source. Where did we come from? Who created us? Why were we created?

We know that God is our Source and we came from Him. To know about us and the purpose of creation, we need to understand who our God is. We were created to function like God functions. Sometime in eternity past, God decided to create the planet Earth to expand His kingdom and territory.

To manage that planet, He decided to create a species in His image and likeness.

When God created Adam, the life of Adam came from God. His body came from the earth, but his spirit came from God Almighty. When God breathed into man's nostrils, the very DNA, or essence, of God went into Adam. If we take the DNA of our spirit and the DNA of God and compare, they will have similar codes. Because we carry the DNA of God, we are able to do everything God does, in a minor way.

When God creates something, He defines its purpose. After its creation, He said, "Let it…" or "Let them…" and proclaimed what He expected them to do. This means He was specific about why He was creating it and what He planned for them. God did not leave room for any guesswork. When we read Genesis 1, it clearly states the purpose of everything, and if it is not stated in Genesis 1, we can find it elsewhere in the Bible. We are going to go through Genesis 1 and see the purpose of each created thing.

"In the beginning God created the heavens and the earth" *(Genesis 1:1)*. Take note that the word heaven is plural. That means there was more than one heaven. The Bible clearly tells us there are at least three heavens. Paul writes about his experience of being caught up into the third heaven *(2 Corinthians 12:2-4)*. If there is a third heaven, there has to be a second and a first.

The first heaven is where the birds fly *(Genesis 1:20)*, and where the solar system and the firmament exists. God called the firmament first heaven *(Genesis 1:8)*. The second heaven is where the principalities and the spiritual host of wickedness reside as it says in Ephesians 6:12. The third heaven is paradise. That is where Paul was taken away to. I believe there are more than three heavens. The ancient book of Enoch talked about seven heavens.

The Bible says heaven is God's throne *(Isaiah 66:1)*, but the earth He gave to the children of men *(Psalm 115:16)*.

UNDERSTANDING PURPOSE

In Genesis 1:3, God created light. Light was created to rule over darkness.

In Genesis 1:6, God created the firmament, and its purpose was to divide the waters from the waters.

In Genesis 1:9–10, God created the dry land, which was called earth, and the gathering of waters He called seas. The dry land (earth) was created for us, and the seas were created for the sea creatures.

In Genesis 1:11–12, God created grass, herbs that yield seeds, and the fruit tree whose seed is in itself. He did not specify the purpose of these plants here because they were created for food for mankind and for every other creature, as He mentions later in Genesis 1:29-30.

In Genesis 1:14-18, God created lights and said, "Let them be for signs and seasons, and for days and years; and let them be for lights in the firmament of the heavens to give light on the earth." Their purpose was to rule over the day and the night, and to divide the light from darkness.

In Genesis 1:22-25, God created living creatures in the waters, birds of the air as well as animals on the earth. Their specific purpose for the sea creatures was, "to be fruitful" and "fill the waters in the seas"; the birds were to "be fruitful" and "multiply on the earth; and every living creature" was to do the same in Genesis 1:20-24. Genesis 1:26 says that all these creatures were to come under the dominion of mankind.

Then Genesis 1:26 tells us that God created man in His image and likeness and said, "Let them have dominion over the fish of the sea, over the birds of the air, and over every cattle, over all the earth, and over every creeping thing that creeps on the earth." That is our purpose. Every single human has the same purpose, just as every apple tree has the same purpose.

DISCOVERING PURPOSE, CALLING AND GIFTS

This is very key to understand. We have heard others teach and say each of us has unique and different purposes, and this has confused us. Then they told us to identify our gifts to determine our purpose. That is not the way God operates. He starts with purpose first, not gifts.

Every lion has the same purpose, and every monkey has the same purpose. Every dog has the same purpose, and every cat has the same purpose. There are different types and sizes of monkeys, dogs, and cats. They do not go to school and try to change what they are or become something different from what they were created to be.

Every fish has the same purpose, which is to swim. There are different types and sizes of fish. Human beings collectively have the same purpose, which is to rule and to have dominion over the earth. There are different kinds, sizes, and colors of humans. They were all created for the same purpose.

Then to fulfill that common purpose, each one of us is called to do something different. Our purpose is the same, but our callings are different. Then to fulfill that calling, God blessed us with natural and spiritual gifts.

Once we understand what we are called to do, it is easy to identify our gifts.

God is faithful to grace us with the gifts we need to fulfill what we are called to do. He won't create a bird and then not empower it to fly. He won't call you to do something without enabling you to fulfill that calling. That is against God's nature and character. We will learn more about gifts later in this book.

Take note that every time God created something, He spoke, and it came into existence. When He created mankind, He spoke to Himself. We came from God. He is our Source and our purpose is connected to Him.

UNDERSTANDING PURPOSE

Whatever God spoke over His creation is still true today. They are all doing exactly the same thing He spoke thousands of years ago. None of them has ever tried to change their purpose and God has not changed His mind about any of them. As I am writing this, the sun is coming up on the horizon to rule over the day. The birds are still flying in the sky. The fish are still in the water, and haven't tried to crawl onto the land.

What would happen if you tell the birds not to fly? Can you tell the sun not rise tomorrow morning? What if you tell fish not to swim in the ocean anymore? They would not listen to you. They are all functioning as God created them. Whoever told you that you were not created to rule the earth was from the devil. It was the religious spirit that told you that you were created to sing or to live in heaven.

Everything is functioning as God planned from the very beginning, at least in its present fallen state, except the born-again believers! That sounds ridiculous, doesn't it? The birds are still flying, and the dogs are still barking. Ever since the fall, religiously deceived people have been trying to change our purpose. God never told man He was changing His mind concerning our purpose because we disobeyed Him.

In fact, the opposite should be true. Once we are saved, we should be going back to our original intent. Did you ever see the sun trying to recruit some stars to form a choir in the sky? Have you seen a fish walk out of the water to take over the land? When God created man, He never thought of man doing anything in heaven, nor was it in God's mind that He needed man to solve any problems in heaven someday. Never!

Is the sun doing the same thing today as it did in the time of Genesis? What about other creations? Only in the circus do we see animals doing things that they were not created to do, but that is only

DISCOVERING PURPOSE, CALLING AND GIFTS

because humans taught and trained them to do those things. What about humans? We have been doing things we were not created to do. In other words, we have been performing a kind of circus taught by the devil and his kingdom. The time has come to put an end to that menace.

Just take a few minutes and meditate on it. Everyone in the Bible was following the first mandate God gave to Adam. We should be doing the same thing right now. God never told us to take a break. He never will.

God told man to have dominion over life on earth. The word dominion is a kingdom word. Kings have kingdoms, and kingdoms have dominion. God is a King, and He has a kingdom called the kingdom of heaven. He decided to extend its rule to a planet called Earth. To establish and manage that kingdom, He created mankind and put us here.

To have dominion means to rule, govern, manage, master, establish, be fruitful, restore, work, subdue, overcome, maximize, and cultivate. Each one of us are created to do one or more of the above applications of that word in at least one area of life.

God was very clear and very specific about our purpose when He created Adam. He did not leave any room for guessing or assumptions about why He was creating man and the purpose of mankind. Genesis 1:26–28 is our purpose statement, given by the Creator. *If we do not understand those three verses, we will not understand anything else in the Bible or about life.*

God created man to have dominion over the earth, which means to subdue and rule. Each individual is created to subdue and rule over one area or aspect of life, or they are created to help someone else rule. Dominion does not mean that everyone should become a president,

UNDERSTANDING PURPOSE

prime minister, or governor. It does not refer to taking over someone else's property or governments by force.

If you tell the unsaved or any other religious group that they are supposed to rule and reign on earth, they do not have any problem with it because they are already doing it. The moment you tell a Christian the same thing, they often get defensive. This happens because they have been deceived by the enemy about their purpose.

As long as the enemy can keep God's people deceived about their purpose, he will continue to occupy this planet and accomplish his will on earth instead of God's. He has been successful so far. The time has come for the sons and daughters of God to wake up from their sleep.

When we study the Word of God, we understand that mankind, Israel, and the church have the same purpose, which means there is a common thread all the way through. The same purpose for which God created the first man, Adam, He continued when He planted the nation of Israel and then the church; they all have the same purpose. When Adam failed, He started with another man called Abraham and established a nation. When that nation failed, He chose another group of people to start a different kind of *nation* called the church.

First, He started with one man. Then He chose Abraham and established a nation. Finally, He chose twelve men and established another institution or spiritual nation called the church. They all have the same purpose but different functions. We are going to find out more in the following pages.

CHAPTER 5
THE PURPOSE, POWER, AND FUNCTION OF MANKIND

Everything God created has a specific purpose and particular function. Many people get confused about the difference between purpose and function. Functions are designed to help us fulfill our purpose. However, if we only function and do not fulfill our purpose, we are wasting our resources and our lives. Unfortunately, that is what most people do. They are so focused on their function that they are missing out on their purpose.

For us to function, we need food, air, shelter, clothing, relationships, and various other things. The majority of our time is spent working on how to function better. Only a very few are fulfilling their purpose. There are eight types of major functions that God designed us to do to enable us to fulfill our purpose. We will learn about them in this chapter.

We all have the same purpose and are called to do different things to fulfill that purpose. To help us fulfill that purpose, God gave us different gifts. Just like every car has the same purpose, which is transportation, there are different sizes and models of cars, and they all function differently. Still, the basic principles are the same for every car.

If we focus on the function and don't fulfill our purpose, our lives will be wasted. We have been ignoring our purpose for too long by focusing on the function alone. We are working hard, trying to take care of the family, having fun, eating the right food, trying to help those who are in need, and so forth. They are all part of our function and not our purpose.

What if we had a car and every morning we went out and cleaned and polished it, built the most expensive interior with a solid gold steering wheel, and every seat had video screens built in with every other imaginable gadget in the world? Just imagine that. Then you start the car and leave it on for a few minutes, but you never use that car to take you anywhere. That car is not fulfilling its purpose; even though it is functioning, it is wasting its resources.

That is what happens to many people's lives. They have a good education and working hard. They are functioning and spending a lot of money to take care of themselves. They have all the latest fads and toys, but inside they are still wondering about their purpose.

What is the difference between purpose and function? Purpose is the original intent for which something is created, and function is how we operate to achieve it. Now let's explore the purpose and function of mankind. Some of the following material will appear in my other writings because these ideas are the necessary foundation for the kingdom mandate. Each time you read through it, may that mandate become strengthened in your inner man.

THE PURPOSE OF MANKIND

As we read before, man was created to have dominion over the earth. You need to hold that truth very close to your heart. If you miss that, you will miss everything else about life.

> Then God said, "Let Us make man in Our image, according to Our likeness; let them have *dominion* over the fish of the

sea, over the birds of the air, and over the cattle, over all the earth and over every creeping thing that creeps on the earth." So God created man in His own image; in the image of God He created him; male and female He created them. Then God blessed them, and God said to them, "Be *fruitful* and *multiply*; *fill the earth* and *subdue it*; have *dominion* over the fish of the sea, over the birds of the air, and over every living thing that moves on the earth". (Genesis 1:26-28)

Here, God the Creator mentions His purpose for creating man. Only the manufacturer knows the purpose of a product. It is very important that we understand this. We all have preconceived assumptions taught by the religious spirit, culture, movies, and philosophers, in our heart and mind, so when we read the Word, we assume we know what it means because we read the words, but in truth very few understand it.

We have been taught that God created man to worship Him. This is one of the biggest deceptions of the enemy. He knows that if he can keep us deceived, we will not bother him with the dominion of the earth. We have been taught that God created us to live in heaven. There is no mention of that in Genesis or Revelation. The devil knows that if he can keep us deceived into believing that the earth does not belong to us, but to him, then he can freely misuse it and its resources for his evil intent, and man will not bother him.

God created man to live on this earth and gave him the earth to manage. We are going to reign with Christ, not in heaven, but on the new or restored earth. Our eternal purpose is connected with the planet Earth, not heaven *(Genesis 1:26; Revelation 22:5)*.

Even if we are functioning and living a good life, if we are not exercising dominion over at least one area of life, then we are not fulfilling our purpose. We are wasting all those resources for nothing.

Since dominion means to rule, govern, manage, master, establish, be fruitful, restore, work, subdue, overcome, maximize, and cultivate, each of us is created to rule or master at least one area of life. That is our purpose. Once we recognize that, the next step is to know what God has called us to do to fulfill it. He gave gifts to each one of us to fulfill that calling. Therefore, we need to focus on developing those gifts.

Now let's explore the different functions of mankind. How are we supposed to function in order to fulfill our purpose? I have no room to mention every single function of mankind, so there is no way I can list them all. I am only listing a few that I think are most important, but neglected.

THE FUNCTIONS OF MANKIND

MAN WAS CREATED TO HAVE A RELATIONSHIP WITH GOD AND OTHER PEOPLE

We are created as sons of God. Our sense of worth and identity comes from our relationship with our heavenly Father. Unfortunately, we try to find our identity in what we do, how we look, or where we were born. We received our bodies from our parents, but they did not create our spirit. God created our spirit, so our identity comes from Him. Unless our relationship with God is in the right place, nothing else will flourish in our life. We will always feel an emptiness, like something is missing in our hearts.

We were also created to have intimate relationships with each other. Family life is the best example of that. We are always longing for a close and intimate relationship with someone. That is part of our nature. When any of our relationships are not in order, nothing else will work out well. The number one commandment in both the Old and New

Testaments is to love God with all our heart, soul, and mind and to love others as we love ourselves *(Luke 10:27)*. Everything in the kingdom of God flows through relationship.

MAN WAS CREATED TO WORK OR ACHIEVE

God created the Garden of Eden and put man in it to till it and keep or guard it. Genesis 2 says, "And Jehovah Elohim took Man and put him into the Garden of Eden, to till it and to guard it" *(Genesis 2:15 Darby)*.

It is interesting to see what God asked Adam to do in the garden. One translation says to tend the garden. It means to develop, cultivate, manage, and make it productive. Whatever man found in the garden, he was supposed to do all that with it. He was not only to till or tend the garden, but to guard it. Guard it from what? From any unauthorized visitors or intruders.

God knew the devil would try to enter into the garden, and He warned and prepared Adam for that. As it says in Ezekiel, the devil was in that garden of Eden once before *(Ezekiel 28:13)*. The Hebrew word for "to keep or guard" is OT:8104 *shamar*[1]; properly, "to hedge about (as with thorns), guard; generally, to protect, attend to." We get our English word *watchman* from this word.

It was Adam's responsibility to protect the garden from evil forces entering it. Adam did not pay close attention. Satan disguised himself and entered the serpent and came into the garden undercover. Satan knew he could not enter the garden directly because Adam would have noticed that. He had to find a way to enter, and he found it through the serpent, because the serpent was more cunning than any other creature God had made.

---

1 James Strong, "8106. Shamar," Biblehub.com, accessed January 15, 2019, https://biblehub.com/hebrew/8104.htm

God had warned man by telling him to guard the garden, take dominion over the earth and subdue it. Then God gave him absolute authority over all the creatures on the earth. He gave him dominion, power, glory, and finally He gave man His Word. Man's only responsibility was to keep and obey that Word. (The only command God gave

him to keep was not to eat the fruit of the tree which God said not to eat). As long as man obeyed the Word of God, no power on this earth or in hell or anywhere else could have defeated the man.

What Adam and Eve might not have known was the history of the earth. They stepped into a realm where Lucifer once ruled, and he was not happy that man was now occupying and ruling his former territory, especially the garden of Eden. He became jealous and wanted to take over the earth by any means. To know more about the pre-Adamic world, please read the book **Releasing Kings and Queens to their Original Intent**.

MAN WAS CREATED TO EXPAND AND GROW

The garden was not as big a country as we might think. It was a small area. God wanted man to expand it and make the whole earth like it. That was Adam's purpose, to expand the garden, to grow, and take dominion over the entire earth. There was a river which originated in the garden that divided into four heads and ran across the whole earth.

A river in the Bible is always a picture of the anointing of God or life. Jesus said that from our belly the rivers of living water would flow *(John 7:38)*. In Psalms we read there is a river that makes glad the city of God *(Psalm 46:4)*. Rivers shows growth and expansion, keeping in mind that before the fall, the whole earth was like one continent, the dry land in one place and the sea in another. There is archaeological evidence that bears this out.

THE PURPOSE, POWER, AND FUNCTION OF MANKIND

The earth was divided into different continents only at a later time. We read about it in 1 Chronicles 1:19.

The name of the first river was Pishon, which in Hebrew means "increase."[2] Can you believe God named the first river Increase? He wanted them to know what He was expecting of them, which was to increase. God did not start a lake in the garden to water it; a lake is a still body of water, so it does not flow or increase. But a river flows over every obstacle that is in its path, and you cannot stop it. It is in the DNA of a river to expand and spread forth. God put that river in you. He did not put a lake or a tank in you; you have a river, and it has to flow. It needs outlets.

We are also supposed to grow and expand in our understanding, revelation, and knowledge of God. Do not park your life around an experience or the information you received while you were twenty. You need to learn new things to grow and mature. In our twenties, we don't eat the same baby food that we ate when we were infants.

The river Pishon encompassed the whole land of Havilah, which means "circle," meaning it flows to one region, and then it spreads and goes to the next.[3] Then the Bible says there was gold in Havilah, which is very precious. Bdellium and onyx stones were there, too. There is no mention of any gold in Eden.

If they had remained in Eden, they would not have found these precious metals and stones. They had to move and expand to find the new treasures that God had hidden in the earth. As long as you remain

---

[2] "What Does Pishon Mean in the Bible?" CompellingTruth.org, accessed January 04, 2019, https://www.compellingtruth.org/meaning-of-Pishon.html.

[3] Smith, "Havilah," Biblehub.com, accessed January 04, 2019, https://biblehub.com/topical/h/havilah.htm.

in one place, you will not discover the treasures God has deposited for you and in you. It is God's idea for you to expand and grow.

The second river was called Gihon, which means "bursting forth" in Hebrew.[4] You cannot stop this river; it bursts forth from you. This is the same as when Jesus said, "out of his belly shall flow rivers of living water" *(John 7: 38, KJV)*. The more you give out, the more God will put into you, and you will reach a place of bursting forth. If you keep it for yourself, you will lose it, or God will take it and give to someone who uses it *(Matthew 25:29)*.

The third river was called Hiddekel, which in Hebrew means "rapid."[5] Whatever God does, He does rapidly because it is not by might nor by power but by the Spirit of the Lord *(Zechariah 4:6)*. What we try to make happen in twenty years of effort, God can do in one minute. This river goes toward the land of Assyria, which means a "step."[6] Sometimes all it takes is a step to step into the destiny God has for you. God is waiting for you to take a step by believing in Him.

The fourth river was called Euphrates, which in Hebrew means "fruitfulness."[7] The first commandment of God to man is to be fruitful *(Genesis 1:28)*. That is what God wants from all of us—fruitfulness.

---

4 James Strong, "1521. Gichon," Biblehub.com, accessed January 04, 2019, https://biblehub.com/hebrew/1521.htm.

5 Smith, "Hiddekel," Biblehub.com, accessed January 04, 2019, https://biblehub.com/topical/h/hiddekel.htm.

6 Francis Brown, Samuel Rolles Driver, and Charles Augustus Briggs, "Ashshuwr - Old Testament Hebrew Lexicon - New American Standard," Bible Study Tools, accessed January 04, 2019, https://www.biblestudytools.com/lexicons/hebrew/nas/ashshuwr.html.

7 Easton, "Euphrates Definition and Meaning - Bible Dictionary," Bible Study Tools, accessed January 04, 2019, https://www.biblestudytools.com/dictionary/euphrates/.

Jesus said to go and bear fruit. There are different kinds of fruit that we can bear as a Christian. There is the fruit of our body, the fruit of righteousness, the fruit of the spirit, and even every invention is a fruit of our imagination.

The breath of God that was in man had all these qualities. After the fall, man lost much of his creative ability and succumbed to his own circumstances. He lost the anointing to expand and spread out. They remained in one place and increased in number but failed to expand the kingdom of God.

MAN WAS CREATED TO MANIFEST THE GLORY OF GOD

Man was the only visible form of God on earth. God wanted to live through man so that those who saw man would see God. In this way, God gave us His *glory*. When we hear the word glory, it is possible to have preconceived ideas about what that means. Usually we use and hear the word *glory* in relation to praise or a feeling. That is not the only type of glory mentioned in the Bible. We are created to manifest seven dimensions of God's glory.

1. MAN'S GLORY: GLORY RELATED TO THE SONS OF GOD

Man was filled and covered with the glory of God in the garden. That is our inherent glory. It did not come through worship or by doing anything, but just by being the children of God. It was our inheritance from Him. When we sinned, we lost the glory of God; in fact, the Bible says, "All have sinned and fall short of the glory of God" *(Romans 3:23)*. Because we lost the glory through sin, we lost the capacity to know God, and we lost the capacity to represent Him. Jesus came to restore that glory. Those who believe in Him become the children of God and receive His glory. In speaking to His Father, Jesus said, "The glory that you have given me I have given them" *(John 17:22 ESV)*.

2. SOLOMON'S GLORY: GLORY RELATED TO OUR PROSPERITY

"Consider the lilies, how they grow: they neither toil nor spin; and yet I say to you, even Solomon in all his glory was not arrayed like one of these" *(Luke 12:27)*. What was Solomon's glory? It was the glory of God manifested through his wisdom and prosperity. Solomon was the wisest and richest man who ever lived. Your prosperity is directly connected to the proportion of your wisdom. The wisdom and riches of our God are unsearchable *(Romans 11:33)*. We are created to manifest that on this earth.

3. MIRACLES: GLORY RELATED TO THE SUPERNATURAL

In the Gospels, we read that Jesus manifested His glory through the miracles He did. The first miracle He did was to turn the water into wine. The Bible says, "This beginning of signs Jesus did in Cana of Galilee and manifested His glory; and His disciples believed in Him" *(John 2:11)*.

When Jesus was informed that Lazarus was sick, He told His disciples that his sickness was not for death, but for the glory of God. When He came to raise Lazarus from the tomb, He told Martha that if she believed, she would see the glory of God. When we move in the supernatural power of God, we manifest God's glory.

4. CREATION: GLORY RELATED TO OUR WORK

All creation reveals the glory of God. "The heavens declare the glory of God; and the firmament shows His handiwork" *(Psalms 19:1)*. We are supposed to manifest the glory of God through the works we do. Whatever we do should represent our God. Jesus revealed the glory of His Father through the works He did.

> There are also celestial bodies and terrestrial bodies; but the glory of the celestial is one, and the glory of the terrestrial is another. There is one glory of the sun, another glory of the moon, and another glory of the stars; for one star differs from another star in glory. (1 Corinthians 15:40-41)

When we manifest God's glory through our work, we will fill the earth with His glory as the Bible says *(Numbers 14:21; Psalm 72:19)*.

5. PRAISE: GLORY RELATED TO SINGING

We are familiar with this kind of glory. This is the glory we experience when the presence of God manifests as we sing. It is based on the Old Testament.

6. ETERNAL GLORY: RESURRECTION GLORY AS WE BECOME MORE LIKE JESUS

> So also is the resurrection of the dead. The body is sown in corruption, it is raised in incorruption. It is sown in dishonor, it is raised in glory. It is sown in weakness, it is raised in power. (1 Corinthians 15:42-43)

Paul says our present affliction is nothing compared to the exceeding and eternal weight of glory that will be revealed in us *(2 Corinthians 4:17)*.

> Beloved, now we are children of God; and it has not yet been revealed what we shall be, but we know that when He is revealed, we shall be like Him, for we shall see Him as He is. (1 John 3:2)

DISCOVERING PURPOSE, CALLING AND GIFTS

7. MARRIAGE: REVEALING THE NATURE AND GLORY OF GOD

> "For a man indeed ought not to cover his head, since he is the image and glory of God; but woman is the glory of man" (1 Corinthians 11:7).

When a man and woman come together in marriage, they reveal the nature and qualities of God. Man or woman alone cannot reveal His glory. God is revealed in the Bible as a father as well as a mother.

MAN WAS CREATED TO FIGHT AND CONQUER

Men were created in such a way that they need something to fight for. They need a woman, country, kingdom, or a cause. They need a new horizon to conquer, a new challenge to overcome, a new boundary or limit to break. It's in their nature to fight. They need a king and kingdom to rally behind too.

Almost every nation that exists today was once ruled by a king. Why were kingdoms powerful in the olden days? Thousands of people gave their lives in one way or another for their king and their kingdoms. Man needs something to fight for because it thrills and motivates him.

In our day and time, people still fight for their country. When I say fight, I am not talking about fighting our family members or our neighbors. We need to fight against the kingdom of darkness and the gates of hell to establish the will and the kingdom of our King Jesus Christ.

MAN WAS CREATED TO FUNCTION LIKE GOD

The reason we are created in God's image and likeness is to function like Him here on earth. What God is in heaven, we are on earth. What He does in heaven, we're supposed to imitate or copy here *(Ephesians 5:1)*. The only way we will live successfully is if we learn to function like Him.

"As He is, so are we in this world" *(1 John 4:17b)*. That verse is powerful. "As He is" not "as He used to be" refers to the present state and function of God or Jesus; we're supposed to emulate Him in this world, not the world to come. We have a long way to go.

When Adam fell, we lost the ability to function like God. We became prey to outside forces and circumstances. When we become children of God, that all changes. We can now reflect our King and function in His kingdom. If you'd like to know more on how to function like God, please read the book **Kingdom Family.**

MAN WAS CREATED TO MANIFEST AND REPRESENT GOD ON EARTH

Those who see us should know and see God. Just as Jesus said, "He who has seen Me has seen the Father" *(John 14:9)*, those who see us should see our Father. I am not talking about His physical form but the works we do. Jesus said that people should glorify our Father in heaven by seeing our good works. He was—and is—the exact representation of God the Father. We are supposed to represent God to the rest of creation and the demonic world. One of the purposes of the church is to teach the wisdom of God to principalities and powers in the heavenly places *(Ephesians 3:10)*.

MAN WAS CREATED TO GLORIFY GOD BY ACCOMPLISHING THE WORKS THAT HAVE BEEN PREPARED FOR THEM

How did Jesus glorify His Father while He was on earth? Towards the end of His earthly ministry, He said, "I have glorified You on the earth. I have finished the work which You have given Me to do" *(John 17:4)*. Jesus glorified His Father by completing the works His Father gave Him to do.

Many think they glorify God by merely singing songs. That's not the way we are supposed to glorify Him.

> For we are His workmanship, created in Christ Jesus for good works, which God prepared beforehand that we should walk in them. (Ephesians 2:10)

God has prepared a certain amount of works for each person to accomplish on earth. These are not works people do to look righteous and holy before men and God. (Those kinds of works are called filthy rags in the Bible.) We have to recognize the works God wants us to do, and do them with our whole heart. These works are part of our calling.

In other places, the Bible calls them "good works." Good works are not just helping the poor and feeding the hungry. Anything good that you do, including business, manufacturing, teaching, training, skills, and more are good works. Christians worldwide are focused on helping the poor and feeding the hungry; we should certainly help them, but that is only one type of good work.

Focusing only on those things is a misunderstanding of the term "good works." God did not put us on earth only to help the poor. Christians have neglected other aspects of society and because of that, have lost credibility and trust in the eyes of the public.

All those functions are supposed to work together to complement and help us to fulfill our purpose. It is impossible to list all the functions of a human being. The functions listed above are the major ones God expects from each of us.

THE PURPOSE, POWER, AND FUNCTION OF MANKIND

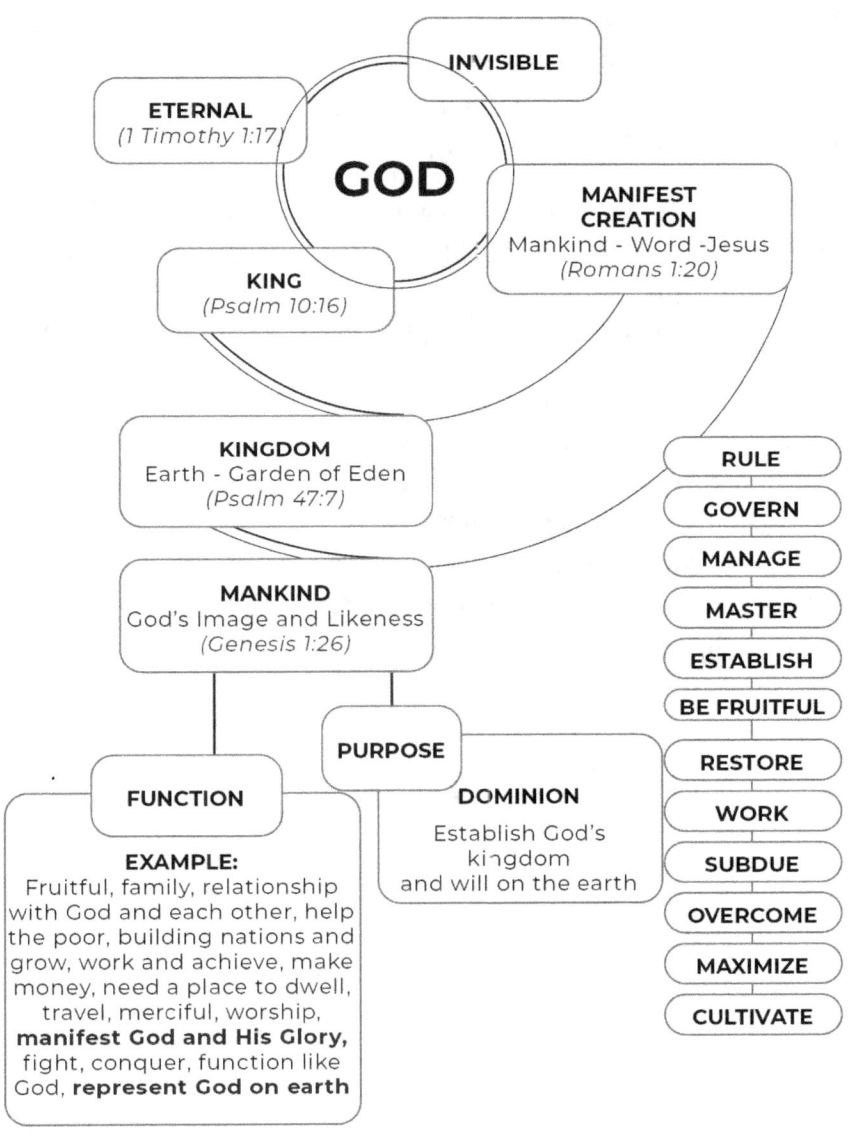

THE POWER OF MANKIND

In Genesis 1:26 we see that in creating mankind, God included Himself by saying, "Let Us make man," but we do not see Him including Himself when He designated our purpose. There, He said, "Let *them* have dominion." I wondered why.

As the Bible says, heaven belongs to the Lord, but the earth He gave to the children of men (Psalm 115:16). *What we do with this planet is up to us.* We can take care of it or destroy it. What we allow or don't allow to happen is up to mankind. We have been given authorization by God to rule it.

That is the reason God won't step in to stop evil things from happening, or override the free will of man. He has given us the ability to choose right from wrong, and to depend on Him or live without Him. I have written a powerful book on the power we have been given called the **Power and Authority of the Church**. I encourage you to obtain a copy and read it.

CHAPTER 6
THE SIX-FOLD ETERNAL PURPOSES OF MANKIND

THE MANY MEANINGS OF DOMINION

The sole purpose of mankind hangs on that single word *dominion*. It has manifold meanings and applications. There are six dimensions of dominion that I like to share with you in this chapter. The number seven is the number of perfection. The Bible talks about the seven-fold purposes of mankind.

> Out of the ground the Lord God formed every beast of the field and every bird of the air, and brought them to Adam to see what he would call them. And whatever Adam called each living creature, that was its name. (Genesis 2:19)

I was both shocked and blessed to read the above verse and see how much trust the Father had in his son, Adam, to name all of the creatures He created. In this, we see a divine partnership. God created everything, but He gave the responsibility to man for naming what He created. We don't see God ever correcting or interfering with Adam's responsibility to name the millions of creatures He created. The question is, why?

God gave Adam absolute authority to name those creatures whatever he wanted because **everything related to the earth realm had**

been committed to Adam's (mankind's) jurisdiction. That is an important kingdom principle to understand. It means that when it comes to the planet earth, it is mankind's responsibility to decide what should and shouldn't happen.

What is jurisdiction? *Jurisdiction* **refers to the official power to make legal decisions and judgments, or the territory or sphere of activity over which the legal authority of a court or entity extends.**

Whatever Adam called each living creature, that became its name because God gave the authority to mankind to decide what needs to happen when it comes to the earth realm. We are still calling those creatures by the names Adam named them. God and man worked in a very clear and defined partnership. There was no confusion about what each one's role was. God did His part and then handed it over to man to continue from there. There was no confusion and no stepping over the other's responsibility.

We have often blamed God or the devil for what is happening on the earth without realizing who is responsible for it. Many say God is in control and wash their hands from their God given responsibility. You might say, Abraham, that is the Old Testament. In the New Testament, we have been commanded to sing and take some people to heaven with us. Really? I want to show you what the New Testament says about who is entrusted with the jurisdiction over the earth realm.

> I will give you the keys of the kingdom of heaven; the things you don't allow on earth will be the things that God does not allow, and the things you allow on earth will be the things that God allows. (Matthew 16:19 NCV)

The verse above is the clear direction given to the church by Jesus Christ. The same thing God told Adam in Genesis, He told the church in the New Testament. God's purposes never change; they are eternal.

There's no point in saying that God is in control. He is not in the controlling business.

Even today, mankind is making decisions regarding what is happening on the earth. Sadly, the wicked are in positions to make the majority of the decisions while the righteous complain about those decisions and the consequences they bring. This must change.

All of creation is waiting for the manifestation of the sons of God. Why? Because creation recognizes the sons of God and the responsibility that has been vested in them by God. Sadly, the sons of God these days don't recognize it. They have fallen into a deep sleep. They are waiting to evacuate or to fly away. That's what they have been taught by the religious system. It is time for the sons of God to rise up in every nation and take our rightful place.

Our Father wants us to partner with Him in accomplishing His kingdom assignment on the earth. Below is a prayer that will help us do just that.

> Dear heavenly Father, thank You so much for giving me Your kingdom and creating me as a king on this earth. Open my eyes to see and receive the mysteries of Your kingdom. Please make me a part of what You are doing on this earth right now. I dedicate my life and everything I have to establish Your kingdom, for Your purpose, to see Your will done on earth as it is in heaven. In Jesus Christ's holy name, I pray. Amen.

1. FUNCTION AS A GATE OF HEAVEN – AGAINST THE GATES OF HELL

A gate is something that gives or denies access. We are supposed to be giving God and His kingdom access to operate on the earth and, at the same time, denying the devil and his demons from gaining any rights to operate on the earth. That's what we are supposed to be doing as gates.

People and places that we dedicate to God function as a gate of heaven on the earth. If we buy a piece of land and dedicate it to the service of the Lord or invite Jesus our King to come and establish His reign over that spot, heaven will hear it, and portals will be established between that place and heaven from that point.

This means that there will be an open heaven above that ground or building. It is called a gate of heaven from that point on. Since humans are the ones who received the right from God to rule the earth, we have the authority to give or deny God permission to operate or rule the earth.

Remember when the people of Israel went to Samuel and asked him for a king like other nations. Samuel asked God, and He told him to heed the voice of the people because they did not reject Samuel, but God from reigning over them. That means mankind can deny or stop God from reigning over them or the earth *(1 Samuel 8:7; Mark 5:17-18; John 19:15)*.

2. PROVIDE GOD THE LEGAL ACCESS TO OPERATE ON THE EARTH – BODY OF CHRIST

When God created us, He included Himself in the creating part, but when He gave the right to rule the planet, He did not include Himself. He said, "Let them have dominion…" That pronoun *them* represents the entire human race, comprised of both male and female.

God gave us the absolute right to rule this planet. Ever since He limited Himself to work in partnership with mankind in everything that needs to happen on the earth. We have the authority to decide what should and shouldn't happen on the earth. As read above, we are the gatekeepers. We can open the doors in the spirit for God or the demonic world and allow them to operate on the earth.

We have the freedom to choose to serve God, the devil, or ourselves. Unfortunately, mankind chose to open the door for the demonic world and gave them the right to rule this planet through them. There are more people on earth today who have given themselves to do the will of the devil, so they give him permission to do whatever he wants to do on the earth.

When man chooses to partner with the devil to accomplish his evil will, God won't override our choice in order to stop the devil or us. We gave the devil the right to do everything he is doing, so God is not responsible for it.

There is only one force on the earth that can stop the devil from what he is doing, and that force is mankind. When we wake up to our true identity and the rights that God gave us, the devil and his kingdom will be history. Until then, he will continue working his evil plan.

When God created us, He did not bring a body from heaven and drop us off here. He came down and formed our body from the earth. Earth is a physical or visible realm, and spirits are invisible and made of materials that cannot be seen with our natural eyes.

For any spirit beings (either God's or demonic spirits) to operate on the earth, they require two things. First, that spirit requires a physical body; and second, it requires the license (legal right) to do business on the earth from the original Owner or Creator. We are the only authorized entity by God, that has the legal right to permit or don't permit God from operating on the earth.

God created this planet to be an extension of His kingdom. He wanted to make sure His will and plans are executed on earth as it is in heaven. He cannot dwell on the earth to do that because He doesn't have a physical body. He cannot appoint angels to do it because they don't have a physical body either.

Instead of God living on the earth personally, He decided to take a body from the earth and put His Spirit into that body so He could receive the legal right to be on the earth and accomplish His will. God's expectation was that this species He created would yield themselves to His Spirit and give Him permission and work in partnership with Him forever and ever.

Mankind is the only officially authorized creature by God that has the legal right to do any legislation or to authorize any other creatures or spiritual entities to do anything on the earth. When it comes to this planet, we hold the jurisdiction to decide what needs to happen here.

The problem was that God created this creature with the freedom to choose. Because of the history of the earth before mankind was created, God had to create this species with free will. The devil had access to the earth before God created mankind, so God wanted to see whom this mankind will choose to love and serve, Him or the devil.

It is the fact that we live in a body that makes it legal for us to live and operate on the earth. The moment we lose our bodies, we lose the right to do anything here. We are supposed to leave the planet when we lose our bodies. With our bodies, we are supposed to make God legal in the physical realm.

God's Spirit and demonic spirits are looking for bodies to make them legal on the earth. When a person yields his or her body to an evil spirit, that spirit's evil nature will manifest on the earth through that person. If we yield our body to God and His Spirit, His nature and will become visible or manifest on the earth.

THE SIX-FOLD ETERNAL PURPOSES OF MANKIND

So why isn't God doing what we are expecting Him to do? Why does God seem powerless in the issues of mankind on this planet? Why does the enemy and his kingdom seem so powerful? Because we don't have enough people in those areas who yield their bodies to God to make Him legal to operate in that sphere.

Why is the media world overtaken by evil forces? Why is the political world filled with corruption and injustice? Because the people who are in those spheres have given their bodies to the will of the evil one rather than to God. These people make the demons legal to operate in those areas.

We don't have enough believers who will make God legal in those areas. We are the light of this world. When the light is absent from the political world, darkness takes over and rules that area. When the light is absent from the educational world, darkness takes over and accomplishes their will instead of God's.

God is only able to do what He wants to the extent that mankind will cooperate and partner with Him. That's why the Bible says the eyes of the Lord run to and fro throughout the entire earth, looking for people on whose behalf He can show Himself strong *(2 Chronicles 16:9)*. He can't find too many.

When God visits the church, people are too busy singing to make Him happy. They are too lazy and are waiting to be raptured out of here. He can't find enough willing and trained vessels who will give themselves to do His will. Or they are crying to have some emotional experience and call it a revival.

On the other hand, the devil has no problem finding people to do what he wants to do on the earth. There are plenty of people who sold themselves to do the will of the devil. They are not waiting for the devil to send a "revival" or some kind of special experience. They do this naturally. We are supposed to be doing this naturally as humans. Living out our purpose supposed to be natural.

That is why we are called the body of Christ. It means we make Christ legal to operate on the earth, at least we are supposed to. Without us, Christ cannot do what He wants to do on the earth because we are His body. Without a body, a spirit is powerless—it doesn't matter how much power it possesses. A body makes a spirit visible and legal in the natural.

As a body, we have limited Christ in what He can and cannot do. He is a King, and there are not very many bodies to allow Him to rule through them as King to manifest His rulership in the nations of the world. Christ is a healer; but few people allow Him to manifest His healing power through them.

If Christ needs to manifest anything to this world, He needs bodies who are yielded to His Spirit. Each member of the body of Christ is supposed to provide Him with his or her body to do whatever He chooses to do. That's how God's will gets done on earth as it is in heaven. Christ is the revealed will of God. He is the Last Adam. *(1 Corinthians 15:45)*. God sent Christ, who is Spirit, to the earth, and Mary provided a body for Him by giving birth to a child called Jesus.

We were taught that God wanted to hear us sing from the earth. That is not the reason He put us down here. He did not have to give us a body to do that. Angels can sing better than us, and they are doing it 24/7.

3. RULE THE EARTH – DISCIPLE NATIONS

Ruling the Earth means any position of authority or rulership on the earth is supposed to be occupied by God's children, including political and governmental positions. God never intended for any unrighteous to rule this planet. He originally gave the right of rulership to His son Adam in Genesis.

The righteous are supposed to be the prime ministers, presidents, and cabinet ministers in every country. They are supposed to be the governors, mayors, and city council members in every city and state.

That is why the Bible says when the righteous are in authority, people rejoice, but when the wicked rule, people groan *(Proverbs 29:2)*. We are supposed to be occupying the entire planet, so the enemy doesn't get a foothold anywhere. Unfortunately, we left the door wide open, and the majority of the people are sold out to do the will of the evil one.

I couldn't find a single verse in the Bible that says we are not supposed to rule now. God's purposes are eternal and He never told us to take a break from what He initiated in Genesis chapter 1.

4. MAXIMIZE AND MANAGE THE RESOURCES OF THE EARTH

The earth is filled with potential and resources that God deposited for us to use. We have been sowing and reaping from the earth since the beginning of time and haven't exhausted its potential. The earth has been feeding the entire creation for this long, and there is plenty left.

We have been extracting gold, diamonds, and other minerals for centuries. One thing we need to understand about the earth and how it operates is that we need to put a demand, or use our creativity, to get what we want from it. We won't find gold or diamonds lying around; we need to dig them out. We need to exert energy and creativity to get the products we want from the earth.

Every product that we use today came out of the earth. Airplanes, cars, spaceships, clothes, shoes, and houses were all made with materials found from the earth. It is up to us what we want to make from the earth.

If we do not exert energy and creativity, we won't receive much from the earth. One problem with the believers is that they wait for a miracle to happen while the ungodly are out there using their potential and creativity to make what they want. They prosper while the believers survive—waiting for the next miracle.

Sons of God don't live by miracles and signs. Miracles and signs are for unbelievers to bring them to the kingdom. Once we come into the kingdom, we must discover our purpose, calling, and gifts and live by them.

Believers are one of the laziest groups of people on this planet. They do not develop their potential or their gifts. They want something for free. They want God to do the things *they* are supposed to be doing.

5. PROTECT THE EARTH FROM SATANIC INTRUSION

God never wanted Satan and his demons to have any rights to operate on the earth. It was man's responsibility to keep them from gaining any rights. The devil knew very well that if he needed to receive the right to do anything on the earth, he would have to get it from mankind because God gave the earth to man to rule and manage.

That is why God told Adam to take dominion over everything He created. He told Adam that if he noticed any rebellion or usurping from any creatures, he is supposed to subdue them and keep them where they belong. That is why the enemy came to Eve with the temptation. He knew he couldn't receive it the right way, so he came up with a deception.

Mankind fell for the deception, and the devil stole the right (our birthright) to rule the planet from us. That is why even today, the righteous feel like they don't have the right to rule the planet. The wicked and the unrighteous don't feel that way. They will take over and rule any nook and corner of the earth.

The reason the wicked and the unrighteous feel it's a natural thing for them to rule the earth while the righteous feel like they don't belong here is because we have been robbed off of our rights, and many are not willing to take it back. Meanwhile, the enemy continues to empower his seed to rule.

The enemy will keep going with his evil plan until the righteous wake up and receive their birthright from their Father and take their place. Through the death and resurrection on the cross, Jesus received back ALL the authority in heaven and on the earth. Now He is the only Person who has the right to rule this earth. He is the legal heir of this planet. He can only do that through us because we are His body.

But the problem is that He is not on the earth in His physical form. We are His physical manifestation on the earth. If He has to do something in the earth realm, He has to use one of us. That is why we are called the body of Christ. Only through us can He exercise His authority on the earth.

6. GLORIFY AND WORSHIP GOD

This is our favorite part. We love to glorify and worship God. But only a few understand what it really means. Glorifying God doesn't mean we wake up and say "glory to God or walk around saying "glory to God." That is not the way to glorify Him.

We glorify Him when we finish the work He gave us to do. Jesus said to His Father in John 17:4, "I have glorified You on the earth. I have finished the work which You have given Me to do." Each of us is sent down here with a specific task to be accomplished for God's kingdom.

That's why the Bible says we are His workmanship created in Christ Jesus unto good works which God ordained them before the world began *(Ephesians 2:10)*. Jesus did not go around glorifying His Father through singing. His focus was to finish the task He was sent here to do.

Many people also misunderstand worship. We think worship means singing slow songs or having an emotional feeling when we sing. I have written about this in another chapter called Understanding Worship.

We made worship so cheap and meaningless. We don't understand the value or the depth of it. We are created to worship God with everything we have, not through lip service by singing three songs once in a while. Our entire life belongs to Him. We are supposed to worship Him with our life.

We are commanded to love God with all our heart, soul, mind, and strength, not just ten percent or for a two hours on a Sunday morning.

THE SOVEREIGNTY OF GOD AND THE FREEWILL OF MANKIND

Many people have the assumption that God is sovereign, so He can do whatever He wants to do. Yes, He is sovereign; that is why He gave mankind the right to rule the earth. If God decides each and everything that happens on the earth, then we don't have any free will at all.

Our free will and sovereignty of God are supposed to work in partnership. This means, He set things up in His sovereignty, and we have the freedom to choose it or reject it. God will not force or control us. That is against His nature. Sovereignty means ultimate authority, not controlling power.

God set His will and plan in the beginning, and man had the free will to choose God's plan and will or choose the devil and his ways. Man chose the devil and his ways. We cannot blame God for our choices. He already knows the decisions we will make, but the majority of the time, He will not interject Himself to influence us. When the people of Israel reached the Promised Land, God told them through Moses to choose life or death, blessing or curse. It was their choice to serve Him or rebel against Him.

Again, through the deception of the enemy, the people of Israel made the wrong choices. They rebelled against God and received the consequences of their choices. Instead of blessing, they inherited curses.

Earth and life are like an automobile. Once we buy a car, it's up to us to either take care of it or destroy it. We can crash that vehicle or burn it down, or when something goes wrong, fix it and take care of it. It is the same way with the earth. God gave it to us. We can protect and take care of it, or destroy it—it's our choice.

Another picture is like a toy we give to our children. They can play with it and take care of it, or they can break and destroy it. It was our choice to give them the toy; it is their total responsibility to take care of it. Little children and toddlers may not understand the value of it.

It's the same way with planet Earth. Most won't have the maturity to understand the value of the treasure God has given to us. They are like toddlers; they just want to have some fun—and they end up throwing away their life.

CHAPTER 7
OUR ORIGINAL ASSIGNMENT

Genesis 1:26 is one of the most important verses in the Bible, one that every believer should memorize. We should teach it to our children first—even before John 3:16 or any other verses. It is lesson number one. If we do not understand what it contains, we will miss the entire purpose of our existence on earth. This single verse contains the intent of the Creator for creating us as a species.

> Then God said, "Let Us make man in Our image, according to Our likeness; let them have dominion over the fish of the sea, over the birds of the air, and over the cattle, over all the earth and over every creeping thing that creeps on the earth" (Genesis 1:26).

God Almighty has hidden the answers to the age-old questions people have been asking in that single verse. It reveals our *identity* (Who am I?). We are created in the image and likeness of God Almighty. Secondly, it reveals the *Source* (Where did I come from?). We come from God because He said, "Let Us create man" and He sent us here. Thirdly, it reveals our *purpose* (Why am I here?). We are created to have dominion over the earth.

DISCOVERING PURPOSE, CALLING AND GIFTS

Personalize and learn that Scripture! Where it says, "Then God said, 'Let Us make man,' we should put our name and say, "Then God said, 'Let Us make (my Source is God) *Abraham John* in Our image, according to Our likeness (my identity as I am just like my heavenly Father); let *Abraham John* have dominion (my purpose) over the fish of the sea, over the birds of the air, and over the cattle, over all the earth and over every creeping thing that creeps on the earth.'" Try inserting your own name as you read the following verse:

> Then God said, "Let Us make _____ in Our image, according to Our likeness; let _____ have dominion over the fish of the sea, over the birds of the air, and over the cattle, over all the earth and over every creeping thing that creeps on the earth" (Genesis 1:26).

Whatever God spoke to the first man is still applicable to every person today. If we are affected by the sin of the first man, then the purpose for which He created the first man is the same for all people. Nowhere in the Bible do we read that God changed His mind concerning our purpose.

Our whole life hangs on three questions, and the answers to those questions determine our worldview and how we live our lives. Every single person who lived on this earth both asked and looked for the answers to these same questions. Some of them found the answers, but sadly, most did not. The questions are: **Who am I? Where did I come from?** And, **Why am I here?** I often meet believers over fifty or sixty years old who are still looking for their purpose in life.

What if we had known the answers to those questions since we were young? What if someone had helped us find the answers to those questions? How dramatically different would our lives and the choices we made be if we had known the answers to those questions? I will answer the above fundamental questions in this book.

OUR ORIGINAL ASSIGNMENT

The biggest crisis today is the identity crisis. Young boys and girls are confused about their identity and purpose, and in some cases, even their gender. It is becoming more common for parents to allow their children to choose which gender they would like to be.

WHO AM I?

The first question everyone needs to answer is: Who am I? Have you ever asked that question to yourself? This is not a question about your profession, that is: What do you do? It's not about your nationality, that is: Which country are you from? It's not even about your race or gender. This question has to do with your identity.

The Bible calls the first man, Adam, a "son of God" *(Luke 3:38)*. You are a child of the Most High God. Your spirit carries the DNA of God. The Bible says we are created in the image and likeness of God. What exactly does that mean? Does God look like us, with two feet and hands? Not really.

God came down to earth to create us. When He created us, everything that He is, went into the man He was creating. That means we contain the same qualities that God has, just on a smaller scale.

God is the Creator, and we can imagine and create. He is Wisdom, so we have wisdom. He is Love, and we can love. He is the King, and we are kings. He is compassionate, and we can be compassionate. He is all-powerful, and we are powerful as well. He forgives, and we can also forgive. He is creative, and we are creative. He is Spirit, and we are a spirit being. He is eternal, and we are eternal. The list goes on. That is what it means when the Bible says we are created in the image and likeness of God.

What God is in heaven, we are supposed to be on the earth. The devil doesn't want us to know or believe this truth. He wants to tell us that we have to do something to become like God. That was the first lie he ever sowed into humans in the garden of God: If you eat the fruit of the tree that God said not to eat, you will become like God.

Ever since that time, humans try to become like God without knowing they are already are gods on this earth. In church we sing so many songs that say, "I want to be like You," and, "I want to be closer to You," and so on, without realizing we are already like Him, and He lives inside each of us if we are born again.

When we are born again, we are recreated in His image and likeness *(Colossians 3:10)*. That is why the Bible says, "As He is, so are we in this world." *(1 John 4:17)*.

WHERE DID I COME FROM?

The second question we need to answer is: Where did I come from? The Bible clearly tells us that we existed prior to our birth on earth. God told Jeremiah that He knew him before He was formed in his mother's womb *(Jeremiah 1:5)*. How did God know him, and where was he at that time?

Ephesians 1:3 says that God has chosen us in Him before the foundation of the world. If we only existed when we were born here, how could He choose us? Again it says in 2 Timothy 1:9 that God saved and called us before time began. These verses and many others prove that we existed prior to our arrival on the earth.

We were in God before we were born here. We were with Him in heaven. Then God knew the exact time and place where He wanted to release us to this planet to fulfill His purpose. It's not an accident that we are here on Earth, our birth is not a mistake. It doesn't matter the circumstances through which we were conceived or born. Even those crazy circumstances have its own reason and intent.

OUR ORIGINAL ASSIGNMENT

We come from God. We come from heaven and the kingdom of heaven. God saw a problem on this earth that needs to be solved, so He designed each of us with specific gifts, talents, and shapes that make each of us very unique. We get into trouble when we try to compare ourselves with someone else who was sent to fulfill or solve a different problem than we are intended to.

God wanted to release a product, an idea, or help create something that other people need, so He chose you and me before the foundation of the world. This is not Calvinism; the truth is that every one of us was called, not just a certain few. But not everyone will realize and receive the plan God has for them. Like the Bible says, many are called, but only a few are chosen *(Matthew 22:14)*.

God sent us to this planet to accomplish a mission for Him. We are not our own. We did not come here to live our own lives the way we want. We have just enough time to complete our mission and then enter into the next phase of life, which is to die and receive our glorified body, and then come back to earth and continue that same mission.

You are an eternal being, and so is your purpose! The works we do now will follow us into eternity *(Revelation 14:13)*. We will receive a reward for our works, and the next phase of life will be based on that reward. Jesus died on the cross and gave His life for us. What was the reward for it? The Father exalted Him above every other name, far above principalities and powers, and the life that He lives now and in all eternity is the reward for what He did while He was on the earth. The same principle applies to our lives.

WHY AM I HERE?

When a manufacturer produces a product, they come up with a statement about the purpose of that particular product. When God created man, He clearly outlined His purpose for mankind too. Genesis 1:26 is that purpose statement. It applies corporately to the entire human race, and it also applies to us individually. Each individual should exercise dominion over at least one aspect of creation; that is his or her personal purpose.

There is much debate and confusion among Christians on the subject of dominion. Many are afraid to talk about it or have never even heard of it. Can you imagine being afraid to talk about the very reason God created us? It's like a bird being afraid to talk about flying.

Many preachers and believers are afraid to talk about the kingdom of God, though that is the subject Jesus preached on the most. Is there a greater deception than this? In Genesis 1:26–28, God makes very clear to us what He meant by having dominion and how to do it. He wants us to exercise dominion on three levels.

First, God wants us to rule the earth for Him. The first chapter of the Bible and the last chapter of the Bible say the same thing concerning man's purpose *(Genesis 1:26; Revelation 22:5)*. Adam was the first king, and God gave the entire earth to him *(Psalm 115:16)*. We are created as kings and priests. After Adam, his sons are the heirs of this earth.

Second, God wants us to have dominion over the spirit world. That is why He told Adam to subdue and rule over the fish, birds, cattle, and creatures that creep on the earth. How could they be any threat to him before the fall? Why would he have to subdue them? God was preparing Adam for a possible assault from the enemy kingdom by using any of those. Satan and his demons were already here on earth before Adam was created.

Third, God wants us to have dominion over the vast resources and treasures He put on this earth. The first commandment God gave to us was to be "fruitful" *(Genesis 1:28)*. Man is made of three parts—spirit, soul, and body. God wants us to be fruitful in all three areas of our lives.

OUR ORIGINAL ASSIGNMENT

The fruit of our body is our children and the works we do. The fruit of our spirit is our spiritual children and the list mentioned in Galatians 5:22–23. The fruit of our soul is the products and ideas we come up with in our imagination to extract and use the resources God put on the earth. If you want to know more about this, please read the books **The Three Most Important Decisions of Your Life** and **Releasing Kings and Queens to their Original Intent.**

The word *human* comes from the Greek word *humas,*[8] which means "dirt" or "of the earth." God took man from the earth and breathed His spirit or *pneuma*[9] into him, thereby making man an eternal being like God. Part of man was taken from the earth, and part was imparted from God Himself. We are a combination of earth and heaven, natural and spiritual at the same time. We are spirit beings living in an earthly (the dirt part) or physical body.

The devil deceived the church and stole what is rightfully ours. We blame Adam for what he did, but we continue in the same behavior. We allow the devil to steal what our heavenly Father gave us, especially as this relates to the earth and its vast resources.

Who is using the majority of the resources our heavenly Father deposited here for our use? It's not His children, and it's not being used to establish His kingdom. The wicked are using those resources instead. An immense amount of money from the oil wells in the Middle East is being used to support terrorist organizations. What a sad situation! In many countries, the majority of the wealth and money the government gains is swallowed up by corrupt politicians, so it never

---

[8] James Strong, "5209. Humas," Biblehub.com, accessed January 18, 2019, https://biblehub.com/greek/5209.htm.

[9] James Strong, "4151. Pneuma," Biblehub.com, accessed January 18, 2019, https://biblehub.com/str/greek/4151.htm.

DISCOVERING PURPOSE, CALLING AND GIFTS

reaches the people who are in need, nor is it used for the development of those nations.

We have been brainwashed by a religious spirit that has convinced us that the earth and its resources do not belong to us and we do not belong here. Instead, many believe we are just passing through. It has been more than two thousand years since Jesus left the earth. What if we have another hundred years or more left before He returns? Are we only going to sit around and sing every Sunday morning? Lord, have mercy!

The wealth and resources that belong to our Father are part of our family inheritance, and they are being used for every wicked thing imaginable and unimaginable while we act like paupers. We need to change this.

> The heaven, even the heavens, are the Lord's; but the earth
> He has given to the children of men (Psalm 115:16).

> "The silver is Mine, and the gold is Mine," says the Lord of
> hosts (Haggai 2:8).

What if a thief came and was illegally living on your father's property? Would you ignore that and let him do whatever he wanted with your inheritance? Or would you go to the authorities and start the process to evict him? In many parts of the world, people take the law into their own hands when something like that happens. They feel violated and angry and then go to the authorities later. But Christians worldwide have been ignoring the devil and his abuse of our inheritance for too long. They are continually waiting for God to show up to fix things for them.

God already showed up in a human body two thousand years ago and judged the god of this world *(John 12:31, 16:10–11)*. That was the greatest manifestation of God on earth. He gave us the authority, power, and keys of His kingdom to undo all the works of the devil. Unfortunately, we are waiting again for God to show up in our meetings to do things for us instead of doing things ourselves.

THE EARTH AND THE WORLD BELONG TO US

Jesus said, "Blessed are the meek, for they shall inherit the earth" *(Matthew 5:5)*.

> For evildoers shall be cut off; but those who wait on the Lord, they shall inherit the earth (Psalm 37:9).
>
> But the meek shall inherit the earth, and shall delight themselves in the abundance of peace (Psalm 37:11).
>
> For those blessed by Him shall inherit the earth, but those cursed by Him shall be cut off (Psalm 37:22).
>
> The righteous shall inherit the land, and dwell in it forever (Psalm 37:29).
>
> Wait on the Lord, and keep His way, and He shall exalt you to inherit the land; when the wicked are cut off, you shall see it (Psalm 37:34).
>
> Therefore let no one boast in men. For all things are yours: whether Paul or Apollos or Cephas, or the world or life or death, or things present or things to come—all are yours. And you are Christ's, and Christ is God's (1 Corinthians 3:21–23).
>
> If we are waiting to go to heaven, when are those verses to be fulfilled?

God did not ask Adam to sing to Him. He told him to have dominion. He is not happy with our *worship* if we disregard the first mandate He gave to us. Praise, composed of music and singing, did not start until almost a thousand years after man was created. If worship was our purpose at creation, what did those people do with their lives for those first thousand years? Instead of singing, they had dominion over the earth.

It was Cain's descendants who invented musical instruments for the first time.

> Then Lamech took for himself two wives: the name of one was Adah, and the name of the second was Zillah. And Adah bore Jabal. He was the father of those who dwell in tents and have livestock. His brother's name was Jubal. He was the father of all those who play the harp and flute. And as for Zillah, she also bore Tubal-Cain, an instructor of every craftsman in bronze and iron. And the sister of Tubal-Cain was Naamah (Genesis 4:19–22).

David introduced worship as we know it today. But if you study the life of David, you will find that he established a kingdom before he appointed singers. Of course, he praised God personally and he was a musician; that was his gift. However, when he sang and said, "Lord, we give you all the glory, power, wealth, and riches," he actually had all those things to present before God. *We copy his songs without ever practicing what he did for God and have nothing valuable to present before the King.* He is not looking for empty words from our mouths. He is a King and He is looking for people who will bring honor to His name, a people living a lifestyle of the kingdom.

God's first order was to have dominion, then to worship, and third, to praise. We have turned it upside-down. Today we try to praise and we call it worship, without having any dominion or anything to show. It is time to change.

Adam disobeyed God, and sin came into this world, so God sent His Son, Jesus, to die for our sins and take us to heaven, right? That's our theology in a nutshell. But there's something missing. What about everything Adam lost because of his disobedience? Adam fell from a particular position and was expelled from a garden called Eden, which was the kingdom of God on earth.

Did Adam fall from heaven? No. If God wanted all of us in heaven, why did He put us all on earth? He should have just kept us all there. Why would He allow His only Son to endure such pain?

CREATED TO HAVE DOMINION

Each of us is created to have dominion over at least one area of life; maybe music, science, the arts, juggling, cooking—it could be anything. There are millions of aspects of life. God wants each of us to be a king over something, which means to rule over something He created. He wants us to imitate Him because we are His children. If there are eight billion people on the earth, each of them is created to have dominion over at least one area of life. There will be many singers, accountants, politicians, clerks, sales associates, and so on.

What is dominion, and how does a person exercise it? The first step in having dominion is discovering your purpose. Dominion is not taking over businesses and governments by force. That's domination. God did not create us to dominate but to have dominion.

There is much misunderstanding about the kingdom and dominion. Man lost his dominion because of disobedience and became a slave to his surroundings and to sin, so God decided to restore man and his dominion. That is why He sent Jesus Christ to this earth.

And so it is written, "The first man Adam became a living being." The last Adam became a life-giving spirit (1 Corinthians 15:45).

God sent Jesus (the Last Adam) to redeem, restore, and save what the first Adam lost.

As His people, we need to be restored to our original purpose and assignment so that we can restore nations to God. If we ignore the first mandate God gave us, then nothing else will work well for us. Everything should be built on the foundation of our purpose, which is to have dominion. If the foundation is not laid right, then the whole structure will malfunction.

That is what is happening to Christians all over the world. We ignored the foundation and went after gifts and making money. The result is chaos and disorder. We have not been raised to live out our purpose, but rather with a survival mentality. This needs to change.

CHAPTER 8
THE LAW OF DOMINION

What made the disciples follow Jesus? He had no mansion, no estate, no donkeys, no horses, and no servants, not even a place to lay His head. We have no record of Jesus owning anything, but people who were business owners left their businesses and their parents to follow Him. Why?

It was because He had dominion. Though Jesus owned nothing in the natural, He had dominion. In truth, He owned everything. How can a person own nothing but at the same time own everything? Through the principle or law of dominion. Though Jesus owned nothing, He never lacked anything. That is deep enough for us to meditate on for a while.

The apostle Paul lived according to the same law Jesus lived. Listen to his testimony.

> By honor and dishonor, by evil report and good report; as deceivers, and yet true; as unknown, and yet well known; as dying, and behold we live; as chastened, and yet not killed; as sorrowful, yet always rejoicing; as poor, yet making many rich; as having nothing, and yet possessing all things (2 Corinthians 6:8–10).

DISCOVERING PURPOSE, CALLING AND GIFTS

How can a person who is poor make many rich and have nothing but possess everything? It happens through living by the law of dominion. Dominion is a law like gravity. When we learn to apply it in our lives, we will experience the benefit of it. As already explained, everything God created is intended to have dominion over something.

The birds were created to have dominion over the air. The fish were created to have dominion over the water. The trees were created to have dominion over the land, and animals over the forest. And last of all, man was created to have dominion over everything God created.

When you operate and live by the law of dominion, everything is at your disposal. You may not own or possess anything in the natural, but you will never have any lack; all your needs will be met. Very few people ever reach this level because most are trying to get more things in the natural and trusting in the natural. Elijah, Elisha, Jesus, and Paul are examples of people who lived according to the law of dominion.

Isn't it sad that some of us have a problem with this idea? The birds and fish understand it better than most believers. If we could talk to other creatures, they would tell us about our purpose. Some people say we have to wait until the second coming of Christ to have dominion.

Try to tell that to a fish. "Fish, you have to wait until Jesus comes back to have dominion in the water." It would reply, "Oh, I'm sorry. I did not know that, but it's too late now. I've been taking dominion here for a long time now. I thought I was created for it." Tell a bird it cannot fly and take dominion over the air because Jesus did not come back yet. What would be its reply? It's time for us to wake up! *(Romans 13:11)*.

If you tell an unbeliever about dominion, they do not have any problem understanding it because they are already doing it in every sphere of life. It's in the gene of every human being—except Spirit-filled believers, it seems. What a horrible deception! If we are not living a life of dominion, we are not even living up to the standard of an animal. There is nothing worse than that.

In Luke 5, we find the background of when Jesus called some of His disciples to His mission. He found them tired and hopeless. The night before He showed up, they tried to catch fish and could not catch anything. They were getting ready to go home to rest.

The first thing Jesus taught them was to exercise the law of dominion to meet their personal needs. *If we cannot meet our own needs by trusting in God, how shall we believe for God to meet the needs of others?* Anyone who follows Jesus must begin where Adam and the disciples began, by exercising the law of dominion.

Jesus blessed them with the biggest catch of fish of their lifetime, through a test of obedience. They saw in Jesus something they had seen in no other human being until that moment. Though He did not own anything in His own name in the natural, He could have anything He wanted at any time. Fish and nature obeyed Him. He was not influenced by circumstances; instead, He had power over them. He was not under anything or shaken by anything that was happening around Him.

We calculate our blessings by how many possessions we have, how many fish we caught that day, how big our houses are, or what brand of car we drive. At the same time, we have no dominion. People don't even know why they exist on this earth, but they have all these gadgets. They are in a race to get more stuff; therefore, the more they have, the less they are satisfied. This is not the life Jesus intended for us.

JESUS OFFERED THEM REAL FREEDOM

When Jesus called His disciples, He said, "Follow Me, and I will make you fishers of men." What does that mean? I did not understand what Jesus meant by it and why the disciples immediately left their businesses and fathers and followed Him. I thought it meant Jesus was going to make them evangelists to go and make converts: Make them ministers and soul winners, right? Has anyone else ever thought that?

Don't you think they should have at least talked it over with their wives or their fathers before leaving the businesses that provided their livelihood? Shouldn't they have at least found a substitute to help their fathers with the business? The Bible says that as soon as Jesus called them, they immediately left everything and followed Him! They did not bother with those things because they found what they had been waiting for all their lives. They did not want to miss it for anything else.

Peter and Andrew were fishermen. They went fishing at night. I have seen this almost every time I go to India because I live close to the ocean. Around six o'clock in the evening, there's an exodus of fishing boats going into the deep waters of the ocean. They come back the following morning after fishing all night. Though they are in business, their survival depends on whether or not they catch any fish.

Jesus offered them something they had waited for all their lives. Jesus offered them two other things, apart from a kingdom, that every human heart longs for. Everyone reading this also longs for these two things.

What two things did Jesus offer? He offered *freedom* and *power*. These fall in the category of the most misused and misunderstood words in our language, right next to the word *love*.

Why freedom? They were tired of the fishing business. They had worked all night without catching anything. They had no control over their life, circumstances, or the fish. If the fish got into their net, they had some income; and if not, they went hungry. They did not get any breaks, and they had no freedom to do the things they wanted to do in their hearts. If you have not slept all night, what do you do during the daytime? You sleep. But if you have a family with children, there is no guarantee that you will get much sleep. In their hearts, they knew they were created for something better and greater, but they couldn't leave their businesses because their livelihood depended upon it.

Millions, maybe billions, of people on earth are in this category. They are doing something they don't like, but because they have no other choice, they continue to do what they are doing for survival. If they quit what they are doing, they will sink. They are between a rock and a hard place, crying out in their hearts for freedom and power.

Many who work a nine-to-five job are in this category. They know deep down that they are not doing what they were created to do, but they are not free to change that. The hope they had in their hearts for their lives and what they actually do does not match up.

FINDING REAL FREEDOM

What is real freedom? Real freedom is the ability to fulfill your purpose. When you are free to choose what you were born to do, that is true freedom. Even if you live in a free society, if you are not free to fulfill your purpose, you are not really free. Conversely, you could live in the most oppressed nation on earth, but be free inside to fulfill your purpose. That is true freedom. Jesus said whom the Son (not the culture or the government) sets free is free indeed. Until we find freedom in Jesus, we are not truly free.

Many confuse freedom with independence. To be independent means to not want to submit, depend, or be accountable to anyone. This tendency comes from a rebellious and prideful heart. "I am going to do what I want, when I want, the way I want, and I don't care how it is going to affect others." That's pure evil, not freedom. Jesus was the freest person in the universe, but He did not have a problem submitting to His Father, even in the minutest details. How is that possible? The sign of *true freedom is absolute submission by one's choice.*

The disciples noticed that this man, Jesus, was different from others. They did not care if He had a mansion or a donkey. They noticed He was free and that He had power. He had dominion. Below are the signs of a free spirit:

Only a free person can choose to submit. Although Jesus was free, He chose to submit to His Father in everything, even unto His death. Many times, we confuse freedom with independence, but they are not the same.

You are free to let go of what is familiar to you. The Bible says Jesus left equality with God and the form of God, and made Himself of no reputation, taking the form of a servant instead *(Philippians 2:6–7).*

You are free to fulfill your purpose. The sign of true freedom is that you are free to fulfill your God-given purpose. Until then, you are not truly free, regardless of the culture in which you live or the government ruling over you. Jesus fulfilled His purpose, though He was born under oppressive Roman rule.

You are free to take a risk. This is another sign of true freedom. You need to be emotionally free to take a risk for God. Jesus's life story is all about taking risks.

You possess self-control. Only free people are able to control themselves, their passions, flesh, and their responses to their circumstances. You must be free to be led by your spirit. Those who are led by the Spirit are the children of God.

You have the fruit of the Spirit manifesting through you. Activating the fruit of the Spirit is a choice. It is in us. You and I can choose to be joyful and choose to love, but we can only do this if we are in Christ.

You have a very active relationship with your heavenly Father. Jesus only did what He saw His Father doing and spoke only what He heard His Father speak. We can walk in this same manner.

You are quick to repent and forgive. Jesus did not have to repent of anything, but He was quick to forgive. He still is. He forgave us and placed His Spirit within us, leading us into all truth in every situation. He is faithful to bring conviction to us when we need it, so we can constantly grow more and more like Him. Being gratefully aware of this process, we, in turn, are full of compassion and forgiveness towards others too.

You are open to learn new things and ways. Free people are secure and not threatened by others or when others exercise the gifts God gave them. Learning new things is imperative for life in the kingdom. We never stop learning and growing.

JESUS OFFERED THEM REAL POWER

Real power is the ability to influence others and to influence your circumstances. It is important to note that the word used is *influence*, not *control*. Many people get confused between them. They try to control people by using their fleshly power or by fear.

Jesus did not offer the disciples salvation. He did not say, "Follow Me, and I will take you to heaven." Neither did He say, "Follow Me, and I will teach you how to conduct revival meetings." No!

Most of our evangelism has involved scaring people out of hell. I remember approaching people and asking, "If you die today, are you going to heaven or hell?" Some people, afraid of going to hell and wanting to avoid it at any cost, accepted Jesus. Unfortunately, they have no idea what Jesus really offered them. We do not see such evangelism anywhere in the Bible.

DISCOVERING PURPOSE, CALLING AND GIFTS

I do not deny there is a hell, but hell was not the motivating factor Jesus used to cause people to love or follow Him—not even to the rich young ruler. When he walked away from Him, Jesus did not say, "By the way, if you don't come back, I will send you to hell." If someone is going to hell, it is not because God is sending them there. According to Jesus, it's their own choice that takes them there. Jesus said this:

> He who believes in Him is not condemned; but he who does not believe is condemned already, because he has not believed in the name of the only begotten Son of God. And this is the condemnation, that the light has come into the world, and men loved darkness rather than light, because their deeds were evil. For everyone practicing evil hates the light and does not come to the light, lest his deeds should be exposed. But he who does the truth comes to the light, that his deeds may be clearly seen, that they have been done in God (John 3:18–21).

EVERYONE WANTS FREEDOM AND POWER

Every human soul is hungering for these two things. What motivates a person who works from nine to five to leave that job and start a business? Freedom. What makes a son or daughter feel like they can't wait to be an adult and leave home? What is their motivation? Freedom. Unfortunately, many leave home for the wrong reasons and do not really understand true freedom and power.

Why do most people want to be in politics? Power. Why do people aspire to make a lot of money? They think money will give them power. Not necessarily. Healthy power is not domination, control, or manipulating others through fear. Those are wrong kinds of power. Hitler had power and influence, but it was a negative force produced by fear.

THE LAW OF DOMINION

There is only one person who can give true freedom and power to people, and that is Jesus Christ. If we are going to restore this nation back to God, we need to understand what Jesus is offering people, and we should offer them the same. If we are going to win people to God, we must offer them what He is offering: a kingdom, freedom, and power. *We should stop offering people religion.*

Do you think people will listen to you if you offer them the three things Jesus offered His disciples: a kingdom, freedom, and power? They would have to be out of their minds to reject such a deal. That is why the Bible says, "The law and the prophets were until John. Since that time the kingdom of God has been preached, and everyone is pressing into it" *(Luke 16:16).*

If you promise heaven, not very many people are interested. (I have not yet met a single human being who wants to die and go to heaven when everything is going well for them.) "Come to church? For what?" they will say, "You have the same problems I do. Why I should I come to your church?" Jesus did not call people to come to church. He offered them a kingdom, freedom, and power. *And they ran to get into His kingdom.*

What freedom did Jesus offer Peter and Andrew? Freedom from their job—their mundane task of catching fish every night to survive, which prevented them from fulfilling their purpose, what I call their "kingdom assignment." What kind of power did Jesus offer? The power to influence men. He made them fishers of men. Every person likes to have influence and followers, which is why social media is so popular. Influence. How many followers and likes do you get? How many friends do you have on your sites?

Everything in life revolves around these two words: freedom and power. People do crazy things to have freedom and power. Why do men and women prostitute their bodies? Why do people forget all else in pursuit of money? Why do they do ridiculous and sometimes frightening things for fame? To gain freedom and power by their own definition.

Why do nations fight against each other? For freedom and power. Why do terrorist groups like ISIS exist? They are looking for freedom and power, but they misunderstand what true freedom and power actually are.

Freedom allows us to fulfill our purpose. You are not truly free until you are free to fulfill your purpose. When the Israelites were in slavery in Egypt, they were not free to fulfill their purpose. They had to do what their taskmasters told them to do. They had no control over any area of their life because Pharaoh and his taskmasters regulated everything.

They had no power or influence over anything. What we need to offer people is not the gift of tongues. We need to offer what people are looking for: dominion. If we are going to finish the task Jesus gave us, a new breed of believers and ministers must rise up in every nation and across the globe.

First, Jesus offered them His kingdom and righteousness. Then He offered them freedom and power. Who would say no to such a grand offer? People will run to Jesus. The majority of the people on earth are not free, nor do they have any power. Why do men and women show their half-naked bodies in advertisements and music videos? They do it for some sort of power and influence. What do rock stars and gangsters want? Freedom and power. What did Jesus offer the sick man at the pool of Bethesda? Freedom from the slavery of infirmity, which had ruled him for thirty-eight years, and the power to live life.

What did Jesus offer Zacchaeus, the tax collector? He was not doing what he was doing because he felt stealing was his primary purpose.

As soon as he found true freedom, he repented and said he would give back everything he had gained illegally. He discovered true freedom and true power. Why do people lie, kill, and cheat? All for the sake of freedom and power, but they are seeking them the wrong way. They will never discover true freedom and power through those paths. It is only found in Jesus.

What is keeping you as a slave from fulfilling your purpose? A job? A habit? A relationship? Religion? Jesus wants to set you free and offer you true freedom. Don't waste your life any longer.

You do everything to satisfy your innate desire for a kingdom, freedom, or power. For example, we want a nice home, which is our spirit's hunger for the lost kingdom. Then we make it beautiful because of the creative desire within us to be at peace with our surroundings. In that way, we take control over our living space. Doing this is the fruit of our sense of freedom and power over it. These three things—kingdom, freedom, and power—undergird our lives, whether we understand the real reason we seek them or not.

The church was hijacked by a religious spirit a long time ago, and most believers don't recognize it. We don't offer people what Jesus offered. We offer a religion called Christianity or a religious experience, or some rituals or even a gift. That is why more people are turning away from church than coming to church. When you discover your purpose and fulfill it, you will automatically have influence.

THE OLD AND THE NEW ARE THE SAME!

If you read history, you will find out that for a long time, people thought the sun orbited Earth. People believed this was true until Copernicus began to question it. He studied the planets and how they functioned. He discovered that Earth rotates a thousand miles per hour.[10] His writings were carefully published with an introduction that made it clear that this idea was only a hypothesis, and it still took a hundred years for educated people to accept the idea. To many church leaders, it seemed like heresy.[11]

Dear brethren, let me tell you with a painful heart that the church we see today did not exist in the New Testament. We have been taught to focus on rapture and revival, and we have been waiting for them while most of the world around us is going to hell.

Jesus offered the same thing God offered Adam in Genesis. He did not say anything different than what God told Adam in the beginning. Jesus had the same message and offered His disciples the opportunity to take what He offered them. Scripture outlines this clearly:

Genesis 1–3	**New Testament**
God created man in His image and likeness *(Genesis 1:26)*	When we are born again, we are recreated in the image and likeness of God *(John 3:3, Colossians 3:10)*
God blessed them and told them to be fruitful *(Genesis 1:28)*	Jesus blessed us and told us to bear fruit *(Matthew 5:3–9, John 15:16)*
God told man to subdue and take dominion over every creature He had made *(Genesis 1:28)*	Jesus told us to tread on serpents and scorpions and over all the power of the enemy *(Luke 10:19)*

---

10 "Why Can't We Feel Earth's Spin?" EarthSky, December 28, 2018, accessed January 17, 2019, http://earthsky.org/earth/why-cant-we-feel-earths-spin.

11 Sheila Rabin, "Nicolaus Copernicus," Stanford Encyclopedia of Philosophy, November 30, 2004, accessed January 17, 2019, https://plato.stanford.edu/entries/copernicus/.

THE LAW OF DOMINION

Genesis 1–3	New Testament
God created man in His image and likeness *(Genesis 1:26)*	When we are born again, we are recreated in the image and likeness of God *(John 3:3, Colossians 3:10)*
God blessed them and told them to be fruitful *(Genesis 1:28)*	Jesus blessed us and told us to bear fruit *(Matthew 5:3–9, John 15:16)*
God told man to subdue and take dominion over every creature He had made *(Genesis 1:28)*	Jesus told us to tread on serpents and scorpions and over all the power of the enemy *(Luke 10:19)*
God gave Adam the earth as his inheritance *(Genesis 1:26)*	Jesus said the meek shall inherit the earth *(Matthew 5:5)*
God put man in His kingdom, the garden *(Genesis 2:8)*	Jesus came to restore and give us the kingdom *(Luke 12:32, 22:29)*
There was no sickness or curse in the garden *(Genesis 1:31)*	Jesus came to die for our sickness and curse and gave us authority over all manner of sickness and disease *(Matthew 8:16–17, 10:1)*
God breathed into Adam His Spirit *(Genesis 2:7)*	Jesus breathed His Spirit on the disciple *(John 20:22)*
God gave them His Word *(Genesis 2:16–17)*	Jesus gave us His Word *(John 17:8)*
They were clothed with God's glory *(Genesis 2:25)*	Jesus said that He gave us His glory *(John 17:22)*
God instituted marriage *(Genesis 2:22–24)*	When Jesus referred to marriage, He referred to the original marriage *(Matthew 19:4, 8)*
God walked with man *(Genesis 3:8)*	Jesus walked with us and dwelt among us *(John 1:14)*
Adam had unlimited knowledge and wisdom *(Genesis 2:19-20)*	Jesus possesses the treasures of all wisdom and knowledge, and He lives inside of us *(Colossians 2:3)*

DISCOVERING PURPOSE, CALLING AND GIFTS

Genesis 1–3	New Testament
Man had dominion over the earth *(Genesis 1:26)*	Jesus said all authority in heaven and on earth was given to Him In turn, He gave that authority to us He said whatever we loose [or permit] on earth will be loosed [permitted] in heaven; and whatever we bind [or forbid] on earth will be bound [forbidden] in heaven *(Matthew 16:19, Ephesians 1:22)*
God told Adam everything in the garden was freely his	Jesus said, "freely you have received, freely give" *(Matthew 10:8; Romans 8:32; 1 Corinthians 2:12)*
God gave Adam a woman	The church is pictured as a woman
Adam was the son of God *(Luke 3:38)*	Whoever believes in Jesus becomes a child of God *(John 1:12)*
Genesis starts with, "In the beginning" *(Genesis 1:1)*	The gospel of John starts with, "In the beginning" *(John 1:1)*
God's will was done on earth as it was in heaven There was no curse, sickness, poverty, or death in the garden	Jesus taught us to pray the same *(Matthew 6:10)*
God did not ask Adam and Eve to sing to Him	Jesus never asked anyone to sing to Him
A river came out of Eden, parted into the four corners of the earth *(Genesis 2:10–14)*	Jesus said the rivers of living water will flow out of us to the uttermost parts of the earth *(John 7:38, Acts 1:8)*
God told them to multiply and fill the earth *(Genesis 1:28)*	Jesus said to go and make disciples of all nations *(Matthew 28:19)*

Jesus' life and mission were a fulfillment of God's original plan, which we can read in Genesis 1-3. My book, **The Three Most Important Decisions of Your Life**, covers more on regaining our original purpose and would aid you greatly in uprooting the religious spirit from your heart and life.

RESTORING DOMINION

If you study the Gospels in detail, everything Jesus did and trained the disciples to do served to restore the dominion they lost. He started with their personal lives. This is true discipleship.

When they encountered the storm at sea, what did Jesus say when the disciples woke Him up? He did not say, "Oh, my, next time you should wake Me up a little earlier! This thing can only be handled by a person like Me." No! He asked them why they woke Him and told them they had little faith. He meant they were supposed to handle the situation in a different way. He was telling them to exercise their dominion over nature *(Psalm 8:6)*.

How much influence do you think the church has over what is going on in our nation or in any nation? Not much. Why? Because we don't have any power. Why don't we have any power? Because we do not understand our purpose. *Dominion reveals your purpose, purpose gives you freedom, and freedom gives you power.* Only free people can handle real power. Otherwise, power will corrupt them. Jesus asked the disciples to follow Him, and after He set them free, He gave them the power to cast out demons and heal the sick.

We were told that Jesus gave the disciples power to heal the sick and cast out demons first. Then they taught us to go after the gifts. That is a misunderstanding. They did not understand the order. The disciples had to go through a series of training before they could exercise power over demons and sickness. It is even true today. When people try to take a shortcut and go after the gifts, sooner or later, they will short-circuit their lives and ministry.

Now that we know dominion is our God-given purpose, how does each one of us apply this law in our lives to fulfill our purpose? That is what we will learn in the next chapter.

CHAPTER 9
TWELVE DEFINITIONS OF DOMINION

God clearly showed us why He was creating mankind. He didn't keep it a mystery, as many people think. He made it plain and simple, but we missed it anyway. When Jesus said He would build His church, He also made it very clear why He was building His church. We missed that, too.

How did we miss the purpose of those two entities? What made us think that God would create us and then not tell us about our purpose? The discovery of our purpose became a mystery to many. They invented all kinds of gimmicks to help people discover their purpose, but we missed it because of the deception of the enemy and the operation of the religious spirit.

Most of us were taught that God created man to glorify Him, to worship Him, or because He wanted a family. These ideas stemmed from the religious spirit's teaching. It is true that we worship and glorify Him when we fulfill our purpose. We are His family because we are His children—but that is not the purpose of mankind. That is part of our *function*. That's how we relate with Him.

God did not create us because He was desperate to have a family and keep them in a different, faraway planet. Why would He have a family, but keep them on a distant planet? If you love someone, you want that person to be close to you as much as possible. Nobody wants to have a family and then send them far away. If God wanted a family, then He would have kept us in heaven. Why would He send us to this planet? But we function as His family to fulfill our purpose. There is a big difference.

> Then God said, "Let Us make man in Our image, according to Our likeness; let them have dominion over the fish of the sea, over the birds of the air, and over the cattle, over all the earth and over every creeping thing that creeps on the earth." (Genesis 1:26)

This verse reveals the how and why behind the creation of mankind by God Almighty. He created us in His image and likeness. He created us to have dominion over the earth. The word *dominion* is very complex. Kings have kingdoms, and kingdoms have dominion. That word shows that we were created as kings.

The word *dominion* comes from the ancient Hebrew word *radah*.[12] The Holy Spirit has given me twelve definitions of the word *dominion*. Many people misunderstand its meaning. People have come up with all sorts of theologies too, like the dominion now, dominion later, or dominion never theology. This and others are very prevalent in many Christian circles.

The good news is that God never changed His mind concerning man's purpose. We are still created in His image and likeness, and that will never change. Neither does our purpose. Nowhere in the Bible does it say that God changed His mind concerning our purpose.

---

12 "Radah Meaning in Bible - Old Testament Hebrew Lexicon - New American Standard," Bible Study Tools, accessed January 1, 2020, https://www.biblestudytools.com/lexicons/hebrew/nas/radah.html)

TWELVE DEFINITIONS OF DOMINION

The word *dominion* means to rule, govern, manage, master, establish, be fruitful, restore, work, subdue, overcome, maximize, and cultivate. Each one of our callings is connected to one of those definitions.

When we operate in the principle of dominion, kingdom evangelism will be a byproduct. This is how people in the Bible evangelized or witnessed for God. We do not see very many people in the Bible going out into the street and shouting. They simply lived out their calling, using the gifts God gave them because they knew exactly why God put them here. They subdued nations and brought righteousness and justice. That is what they were called to do.

We have too many religious psychopaths who have no clue about the purpose of mankind or their specific calling. They have zeal without proper knowledge. They bring more damage and shame to the name of Jesus and the church than good. If you are called to shout from the street corners, go ahead and do it—but don't do it if that's the way the religious spirit has trained you.

Holy Spirit has given me twelve definitions of *dominion*. I will explain them one by one below.

TO RULE

This is the number one and fundamental meaning of *dominion*. Your number one responsibility is to rule the earth on behalf of God. Not everyone rules the same way. Not everybody is called to be in government. But everyone can rule over something, or at least one gate. Doing this will eventually bring the entire planet under the reign of Jesus Christ our King. That is God's original intent for mankind.

First, we start ruling our own lives: our emotions, body, past abuses, failures, and mistakes. If we do not rule our own life, we will not be able to rule any other aspect of life. If we do, it will be temporary, and we will be crushed by life's challenges.

If you are called to be in politics or government or to be a ruler over an area of your country, then go for it. Never hold back. That is one of the ways we can rule. Not everyone is called to be in politics or to become a prime minister or president, but everyone is created to rule over at least one area of life by using one of the following methods.

TO GOVERN

You might ask: What's the difference between ruling and governing? It's similar to the difference between a leader and a manager. A ruler is someone who is over a region, an entire country, or organization. A person in that position will have other governors under him to help him rule *(1 Peter 2:13–14)*.

In our day, an administrator or a secretary would be considered a person who governs. In Bible times and today, it is common to have governors over states or regions. They work under the federal government.

Like every leader needs a manager, every ruler needs governors to help him or her. You might be called to be a governor for a leader in some level. God wanted us to govern the affairs of this earth for Him. He is the ultimate Ruler and King. We are governors under Him.

TO MANAGE

As God's children, we need to be managers of this planet. We need to manage the resources, nature, and everything else He has entrusted to us. We will need a lot more people to manage this planet. Some people think that there are too many people on earth already, but in reality, we do not have enough. There is plenty of space on this earth that needs to be occupied. The only reason that we think there are too many people is because of our congested cities.

In truth, more cities need to be established. When I travel across nations, I found that almost every one of them has the ruins of some old cities and civilizations that existed within them hundreds or thousands of years ago. Now only their ruins remain. Those cities and towns disappeared, and people moved on and built new cities. Why can't we do the same? It is absolutely possible. It needs to happen. Newer and better cities are yet to be built. All major cities in the United States are not even two hundred years old.

TO MASTER

Each of us needs to master an area of life. To *master* means to become the best in something. Once you master something, you are qualified to teach it to others. A skill, talent, gift, language, subject, trick—anything spiritual or natural can be mastered. When you master something, people will come to you and pay you for your service. When you master something and do it like nobody else did before, you will have dominion and you will never be poor.

Discover the gift or gifts God gave you, and master them so you do them like no one else did before. This is the key to your blessings. Why did I say master a trick? There are people who have mastered juggling. I have seen them do it before huge audience. As the Bible says, your gift will make room for you and bring you before great men *(Proverbs 18:16)*. A mastered gift will bring you income and before great people.

Whatever we do, we need to excel in that area and go to the next level. If you are working for a company, gain every bit of knowledge and skill required for you to excel in your workplace so you can move up to the next level. Never stay in one level for more than three years.

DISCOVERING PURPOSE, CALLING AND GIFTS

The potential God put inside of us is unfathomable. Most of us don't realize it unless we are stretched, trained, and required to grow. Unless we demand it, it will not manifest on its own. It will remain dormant. Right now, we have no idea how many skills remain sleeping in our hands.

With our two hands, we can fly an airplane, play an instrument, write a book, cook a meal, drive a car, or build a skyscraper. It is impossible for me to list everything our hands can do if we train them how to do it. We can also teach our hands bad habits like smoking, which will eventually kill us.

Most people have no idea what they can train their hands to do. They remain poor because they keep their hands idle. Some people don't learn new skills because it takes a tremendous amount of discipline and consistency to train our hands to do or learn something new.

We are constantly innovating. We should never stop improving, never stop learning, and never stop innovating. Believers should be the best employees in every company. They should be in demand, and companies should be searching to hire them because of their productivity and excellence. Others should look at us and feel jealous. That was the case in the Bible days.

TO ESTABLISH

Because we are created in the image and likeness of God, it is natural for us to be inspired to establish something: a business, organization, institution, church, or enterprise. We like to build something to make a difference in the lives of people. It is common for people to feel dissatisfied and frustrated when they can't build or establish something. This is especially true of men when they can't accomplish their goals.

TWELVE DEFINITIONS OF DOMINION

TO BE FRUITFUL

The first commandment from God to man was not to sing, go to church, or even preach the gospel—it was to be fruitful *(Genesis 1:28)*. Our whole life depends on us being fruitful or not. Our prosperity depends on the fruit we bear.

Mankind is made of three parts: spirit, soul, and body. Each of those parts needs to produce fruit. Jesus told us the same thing *(John 15:16)*.

In many parts of the world, people remain in poverty, not because they lack resources, but because they lack ideas to utilize those resources. They are not productive with what God has given them. They are waiting for someone to give them something for free or to grant them a miracle.

TO RESTORE

When we see something out of order, we like to restore it to function the way it was supposed to. Too often today, all that we do is complain about the disorder we are seeing. The whole planet is in the process of being restored. You might be called to restore one aspect of life or an area of this planet. That is the way we put into action the image and likeness of God in us.

God started by restoring and remodeling the earth in Genesis 1. That is the way He manifested His nature and likeness. We who bear the same image and likeness must learn to function like our Daddy. Whenever we see something out of order, instead of partnering with the devil and making it worse or cursing it more, we should partner with God and make it better. God sent Jesus, not to condemn the world, but to save the world *(John 3:17)*.

DISCOVERING PURPOSE, CALLING AND GIFTS

TO WORK

There is a huge difference between work and a job. Many of us are stuck in a job we do not enjoy. A *job* is something that you do until you discover your *work*. Your work is your calling. It's okay to do a job until you are released to fulfill your calling. Jesus was a carpenter. That was His job until the day came when He was released to fulfill His calling, which was His work.

Work is what God ordained for you to do, as we read in Ephesians 2:10. A job is something we do until we find that work.

Moses and David were shepherds until they were released to fulfill their destiny. Most people never get released to fulfill their destiny. They are stuck in a job and their main goal is to just survive. They are afraid that if something happens to their job, they won't have any money and will starve or die.

God gave Adam *work* to do: taking care of the garden. That was not a nine-to-five job; it was a 24/7 responsibility. If the *job* you do is your *work*, then there is nothing wrong with it. For the majority of people, their job might be their work. However, if you are presently working in a particular job but your heart is crying out, saying you are supposed to be doing something different, then you need to explore those possibilities.

Fear is the number one enemy of our destiny. Destiny requires trusting in God and stepping out to obey what He is telling us to do. God gave man work before He gave him a woman or family. Men tend to gain fulfillment from their work. If a man is not satisfied with what he does, nothing else will satisfy him.

Below are some of the differences between a job and work:

TWELVE DEFINITIONS OF DOMINION

A Job	Work
A job is something you do to survive until you find your work	Work is based on your calling, skills, and gifting
A job is based on your education	
A job is based on opportunity or availability	Work creates an opportunity for you and others
A job is something that you do to make money	Work is something that you do to fulfill your purpose or destiny. Money comes to you as a reward
A job is something you do for certain hours of a day	Work is a lifetime assignment
A job is something that you do	Work is part of your being
You retire from a job	You will never retire from your work, not in this life or in the next
A job is something you do for others to help them fulfill their purpose	Work is something you do to serve and bless others
A job is something that you do for a salary	Work is something you do to create wealth, and money follows you as a result
A job doesn't give you fulfillment	Work gives you fulfillment
A job is temporary	Work is something you were born to do

A Job	Work
People can fire you from your job	No one can fire you from your work
A job is limited to a place	Work is not limited to space or time

TO SUBDUE

Whether you realize it or not, the moment you step out to fulfill your calling, things will begin to fight against you. There is a natural law called the law of resistance. Everything will try to oppose you or come against what you are called to do. You will need to subdue these forces. To *subdue* means to make something submit by force.

There is natural resistance from nature, from spiritual forces, and also from humans. We overcome these forces spiritually, especially with humans. We do not fight against flesh and blood. There are times to fight against nature. We need to use the wisdom and knowledge God gave us to prepare, plan, and build certain things to overcome the powers of nature.

TO OVERCOME

As God's children, we have to overcome certain things in life. Everything in this life will try to fight against us, and we need to overcome those forces. Below are some of the things we need to overcome if we are going to fulfill our destiny.

- **This World:** This world is under the influence of the kingdom of darkness. The enemy will try to bring us down by using any of the methods available to him in the world.

TWELVE DEFINITIONS OF DOMINION

- **Temptations:** If you have lived very long as a believer, you know about this already. Temptations will come when we least expect them and from places and sources we do not expect. We need to overcome them by abiding in and speaking God's Word. No one is exempt from temptations; it doesn't matter how anointed you are. What you do with temptations is the key to victory or defeat. Even Jesus was tempted in everything.

- **Persecutions:** We will be persecuted for our faith. If you do anything differently than others, you will be persecuted. To fulfill your destiny, you are required to do things that nobody else does. When you share your faith, you will be persecuted. If you are blessed above others, you will be persecuted. If you walk in your unique calling, you will be persecuted. When these things happen, don't think it's a strange thing or that no one else is facing what you are dealing with. That's a lie. Every Christian will face persecution.

- **Law of Resistance**: Whenever you try to do, achieve, or learn something, you will have to overcome the law of resistance. God has ordained life in a way that if you need to develop anything good, there will be resistance. If you need to build your muscles, resistance is the key. If you need to develop a new skill, the law of resistance will fight against you. You need to determine whether you are going to go forward or quit.

- **Negative Thoughts and Mindsets:** Every one of us deals with negative thoughts and mindsets. They come with our fallen nature. We tend to think way below our potential and capacity. We try to play it safe. We must overcome those negative mindsets and thoughts on a moment-by-moment basis.

DISCOVERING PURPOSE, CALLING AND GIFTS

- **Weaknesses:** We all have weaknesses in one or more areas. Don't blame or judge others for their weaknesses. Jesus told us not to try to take the dust from someone else's eye when we have a log in our own.

- **Satan:** Lastly, we need to overcome Satan himself, especially when we are committed to establishing God's kingdom and *ekklesia* on earth. When we are doing this, we become a target of his assignments. When we hear the word of the kingdom, the enemy comes and tries to steal that from us *(Matthew 13:19)*.

TO MAXIMIZE

Whatever God gives you, He expects you to maximize before He will release you to the next level. Your time, health, gifts, and talents are meant to be maximized. Maximize them where you are instead of waiting for the "big door" to open. If you are just waiting and waiting, the doors you are waiting for may never open.

Maximize the time, resources, and opportunities that are available to you right now. When God sees that you are faithful in what has been given to you, He will open the next door and promote you. No one has ever tapped into the full potential God has deposited in them. We might be using less than five percent of what we can access. According to God's perspective, when we think we have maximized something, we are actually just beginning.

TO CULTIVATE

God wants us to cultivate and take care of this planet. To *cultivate* means to create an environment to bring out the best in something or someone. Our planet contains an enormous amount of potential, resources, and products. We cultivate it to bring out that potential. Everything we need to sustain our life comes from the earth.

TWELVE DEFINITIONS OF DOMINION

God did not create airplanes or cars. He created the raw materials for them, hid them in the earth, and gave us the ability to imagine and make what we need. He did not create furniture, either. Instead, He created trees and gave us the imagination to make furniture that we need from those trees.

We also need to cultivate people. The modern term for *cultivate* could be *coaching*. Coaching is a huge business today. We coach others to help them recognize the potential that God put in them and encourage them to utilize it for God's glory. Sometimes we need the help of others to recognize the strength in us and see what we are capable of doing.

Your purpose will fit into one or more of the above twelve definitions of dominion mentioned above. Holy Spirit will bear witness in your spirit about which definition will fit you the best as a person. Follow His leading, study, practice, and become the best in that area.

CHAPTER 10
NINE WAYS TO HAVE DOMINION

To recap what we have learned so far, making it simple and plain, *every human being has the same purpose.* Purpose is universal. To fulfill our purpose, each of us is *called* to do something different. To empower us to walk out that calling, we were given various *gifts*. *Purpose is the same for every individual, but calling and gifting are not.* They are unique and individual.

We all have the same purpose statement, but because of the deception by the religious spirit, we have come up with all kinds of excuses for centuries to deny that purpose. God created man to dominate the earth and its elements, to rule, to govern, to subdue, to harness, maximize the potential, and have dominion over the earth. The reason God wants us to have dominion is to partner with Him in establishing His kingdom and will on earth. That is our eternal purpose in this life and the one to come. It is through discovering our specific calling and gifting that we find the area and means by which we accomplish that.

Now the question is, how do we exercise our dominion? There are nine ways we need to exercise dominion, depending on the area to which we are called.

DISCOVERING PURPOSE, CALLING AND GIFTS

1. SERVE A CAUSE

There are causes that are worth committing your life to serve. There are many social and charitable organizations around the world, and they all serve a cause. Our ministry had a Vision Center in India where we trained orphans and destitute children to discover and fulfill their purpose. Seeing children who never had an opportunity to go to school become entrepreneurs, learn skills, and become who God created them to be has been one of the best programs we ever accomplished. Everyone who has visited has said they have never seen a program like ours anywhere else. That is just one example.

God will guide you and help you discover a cause, if this is the direction He wishes you to go. Even if you cannot establish a cause, you can support those who are working in a particular area as well as those He touches your heart to serve.

2. SOLVE A PROBLEM

You are created to solve a problem. Jesus solved the sin problem. Bill Gates solved a computer problem. Ford solved the automobile problem. Clothes solve the nakedness problem. If a problem grieves your heart, that is an indicator that you might be created to solve or impact it in some way. Every business out there solves a problem, and people pay money when that problem is solved for them.

3. REDEEM AN AREA

The whole creation is waiting for the manifestation of the sons of God to rise up to their true identity. The creation came under the bondage of corruption because of the fall of man. Jesus died to pay not only for our freedom, but for the whole creation, too. His blood is sufficient to redeem and restore everything that was damaged by the fall. The problem is that most of us don't believe that yet.

We have to learn how to redeem and heal the land as God promised in 2 Chronicles: "If My people who are called by My name will humble themselves, and pray and seek My face, and turn from their wicked ways, then I will hear from heaven, and will forgive their sin and heal their land" *(2 Chronicles 7:14)*. What if each of us left this earth a little better than when we came? That's the awareness we should have; that's the way we should think and act.

4. HAVE DOMINION OVER THE EARTH AND NATURE

As Spirit-filled believers, we have authority over the natural sphere of life. We are not to be dominated by any elements of nature and the earth. Weather, trees, animals, water, and everything around us should function to help us and not be against us. Sadly, scores of people are affected by allergies and things that shouldn't matter today. They say things like they are "under the weather" or blame allergies whenever the seasons change. We are not supposed to be under anything that is connected to this earth. We are supposed to be above all that and ruling.

5. GET ELECTED INTO GOVERNMENT POSITIONS

We should exercise dominion by being elected into a governmental office in our nation. There are many levels of responsibilities in which a person can serve—from being part of a school board to being a county clerk or the leader of a nation. All spheres of authority should be occupied by God's children. We should not leave any room for the enemy or the wicked. The Bible says, "When the righteous are in authority, the people rejoice; but when a wicked man rules, the people groan" *(Proverbs 29:2)*. It's a simple principle. When we neglect the roles we are supposed to play, someone else will pick up those opportunities and fill our place for us.

MORE ON POLITICS

Everyone God used in the Bible was involved in politics on some level. There is a misunderstanding in the body of Christ that says we should not be involved in government or politics because they are of the devil. That is a deception straight from hell. As long as the enemy can keep the righteous out of the government, he has complete freedom to accomplish his will on earth through governments.

It's either God's will or the devil's that will be done on earth. It will be *as it is in heaven* or as it is in hell that is manifested on the earth. It's our choice which one we allow. Only humans have the right to permit or not permit what should or could happen here. Many believe God is in control of everything, no matter what we do. God is in control of what is happening in the affairs of men, *only to the extent we partner with Him*. He set it up that way, expecting us to do our part.

Every day we read newspapers and watch news channels about how the enemy is accomplishing his will and plan on earth. Why can't we do the same thing and accomplish God's will instead? Then we should begin a worldwide news channel and broadcast it. The enemy uses his children to accomplish his will on earth. God wants to use His children to do His will, too. We have been in denial for far too long.

From the first Adam to the Last Adam, all were governmental leaders. God created Adam to govern the earth and Jesus is King of the earth and much more. Jesus is coming to rule and reign. Abraham dealt with the kings of his time. Joseph, Moses, Elijah, and Elisha were involved in politics or connected to the governments of their times too, and so was every prophet in the Bible.

The prophet Elisha possessed influence in the government. When he was staying with the woman, he asked her if she wanted him to speak to the king or the captain of the army on her behalf *(2 Kings 5:14)*.

If anyone is truly an apostolic or prophetic ministry, they have to be connected to the government, at least to their local government. The majority of the prophets of the Old Testament were prophesying to kings or to nations and their destinies. God told Jeremiah that He had set him over kings and kingdoms to root out, pull down, throw down, destroy, build, and plant *(Jeremiah 1:10)*. If you'd like to know more about government and how it should function, please order the book **Kingdom Government** and study it.

6. MASTER A SKILL, SPECIALIZED KNOWLEDGE, OR GIFT

Mastering an area of life, a subject, skill, or ability gives you dominion over that particular area. We master something through practice and research. Whatever we learn or master, we need to maintain. To do this requires that we keep updating our knowledge because everything is changing very quickly.

7. DESIGN OR MAKE A PRODUCT

Another way to have dominion on the earth is to come up with a product or service that is useful to humanity. How many products do you use every day? How many products do you have on your body right now that are made by different companies? Think about how they were invented, produced, and marketed. We can do this, too!

8. RELEASE AN IDEA OR WISDOM TO BENEFIT HUMANITY

Ideas have consequences. An idea can change your life and the world. The idea of the law of gravity changed the world. The idea that sounds could travel through a cable radically changed how quickly the world communicated. What used to take months now takes minutes. Later, the idea that sound waves could travel without a physical cable changed how we live and communicate yet again.

9. SPEAK CREATIVE WORDS

Our words are more powerful than we think. God created everything by His word. He spoke, and it was done. We are created in His image and likeness, and we carry the same capacity on a lesser level.

> You will also declare a thing, and it will be established for you; so light will shine on your ways (Job 22:28).

> For assuredly, I say to you, whoever says to this mountain, "Be removed and be cast into the sea," and does not doubt in his heart, but believes that those things he says will be done, he will have whatever he says (Mark 11:23).

The Bible has a whole lot to say about our words and the results they produce.

IN WHAT AREAS SHOULD WE EXERCISE DOMINION?

OUR OWN LIVES

Dominion should start in our own lives and families first. If we cannot rule our own lives, there is no way we are going to exercise this anywhere else. Our body, emotions, passions and appetites need to be brought under the domain of our spirit. If we do not have this and try to have dominion outside, it will be self-destructive.

THE EARTH AND ITS RESOURCES

God has deposited enormous amounts of riches and resources on the earth. They were put there by Him for us. It takes wisdom, knowledge, and understanding to extract and put them to use, but this is an area of dominion.

NATIONS AND GOVERNMENTS

It is God's desire and plan for the righteous to be in authority. He never intended for any wicked person to rule. When the wicked rule, it becomes unbearable for people.

KNOWLEDGE

Each of us are created to exercise our dominion in at least one area of knowledge. We are supposed to master that area like no one else has ever done before. The vast amount of knowledge that is out there comes from God *(Proverbs 2:6)*. There is no way someone can know everything, but we all can know enough of something. That is why the Bible says to study to show yourself approved in 2 Timothy 2:15.

God gives much importance to knowledge, wisdom, and understanding. You can know whether a person has the fear of God or not by looking at their hunger for wisdom. The Word says that the fear of the Lord is the beginning of wisdom. Wisdom and knowledge are the basis for everything else.

OVER THE EARTH AND THE CREATURES MENTIONED IN GENESIS 1:26

In Genesis 1:26, God told us we are supposed to take dominion over nature and all the creatures He created. That is our assignment from the Creator.

OVER DEMONIC FORCES

We need to keep the demonic forces where they belong. We should not be talking about what they are doing all the time. We should be more focused on what God is doing in our lives and around us. Jesus said in Luke 10:19 that He gave us power and authority to tread on serpents and scorpions and over all the power of the enemy and that nothing shall by any means hurt us. That's dominion over demonic forces.

CHAPTER 11
THE PROCESS OF TAKING AND EXERCISING DOMINION

God created us to have dominion over the earth. There are two applications to this truth. The first one is natural, and the second one is spiritual. The natural application is this: In verse 28, God is explaining how to have dominion. First, He blessed them. Then He explained the process of obtaining dominion, which was to be fruitful, multiply, replenish, subdue and then have dominion. This process is the key to understanding our purpose. Being fruitful means not only having children, but to be productive. God wants us to be continually productive.

God put at least one seed in each of our lives. That seed needs to grow and produce fruit. There is a product in each of us that is waiting to be released. This is the key to your prosperity in the kingdom. When you discover your product or service, you become an essential part of life on earth. God calls it becoming fruitful. Thousands or maybe millions die without ever discovering their seed and their product. The reason for the poverty problem is that people are not productive because they do not know that God has deposited a seed in them.

God put a desire in your heart to do something. That desire is a clue to the seed that is hidden in you. It could be ministry, business,

DISCOVERING PURPOSE, CALLING AND GIFTS

invention, song, a book, music composition, service, talent, even a way of seeing that will benefit others. *There is no limit to the variety of ways God wants to manifest what we have to the world.*

Once you discover your product (or fruit), you need to multiply it; that means you manufacture it. After you manufacture it, you need to fill the earth (or market it) or replenish the earth with that product so that others can benefit from it. The next step is to subdue, which means to take control. That means we must implement a managing system for our business, which will result in dominion over a particular area of life.

When we think of computers, two names come to mind: Bill Gates and Steve Jobs. Why? They have implemented the above principle and took dominion over the computer business. What if Bill Gates and Steve Jobs had sat in their living room and sang, "Amazing Grace, how sweet the sound" all day? Or, "This earth is not my home, I am just passing by"? You get the point. They fulfilled their purpose for which God created them. Every successful business uses biblical principles as their foundation. What about you and me?

You are created to take dominion over a particular area or sphere of life. The seed of God in you is waiting to be released. Do not go to the grave with that seed. You need to discover and reproduce it to bless humanity. Do not leave the earth before you make your mark on the pages of history. The whole earth is waiting for the manifestation of the sons of God, which includes you.

In Genesis 1:28, God blessed them and explained to them the steps to having dominion. There are five steps to having dominion. They are:

BE FRUITFUL

The first thing God told man to do was be fruitful. To bear fruit, you need a seed. Fruit does not grow on its own; it needs a tree or plant,

THE PROCESS OF TAKING AND EXERCISING DOMINION

and that needs ground. It also has to be planted in that ground. In turn, the tree or plant produces fruit that disperses more seed. Also, the tree bears fruit not for it to enjoy, but for someone else.

You are created to be a blessing to someone. Sometimes God does not explain the whole process when He says something. He will tell you the result, but we have to faithfully work through the process. There are multiple meanings to the word *fruitful*. The Hebrew word used for fruitful is *parah*[13], which means to bear fruit, be fruitful, branch off, to make fruitful, and to show fruitfulness.

The general idea of being fruitful is having children, the fruit of our bodies. A process is involved in that, too. A baby does not just appear out of man. The man must deposit his seed into the womb of a woman, and then it takes nine months for a woman to birth a baby.

Man is a three-part being: spirit, soul and body. Each of these parts have the ability to produce fruit. When God said to be fruitful, He was not just referring to the fruit of our body. He was also talking to us about producing fruit in the other two areas—soul and spirit.

Unfortunately, most people only produce the fruit of their body, and the other two areas of development remain barren and do not prosper. If you keep producing only children and do not produce any other fruit, then you will not have anything to feed your children. That is the reason there is poverty in many parts of the world. They produce children, but their souls and spirits remain barren.

The key to prosperity lies in the fruit of the other two parts. At the same time, our soul and spirit cannot function without our body. The fruit of the mind and spirit have to manifest through our bodies.

---

[13] James Strong, "6509. Parah," Biblehub.com, accessed January 04, 2019, https://biblehub.com/hebrew/6509.htm.

A fruit is also called a product. Children are the natural products of our bodies. Just as God has put seed in your body, He also put seed in your mind and spirit. We need to discover and develop our minds if we are going to prosper and fulfill our purpose. The Bible talks about different kinds of fruit.

A fruit is something that benefits others. A tree does not eat its own fruit; it is there to attract others to the tree. *When you bear fruit, it is for someone else.* Others want to eat that fruit, and if it is a good fruit, they will pay you for it. If your fruit (product) feeds or meets any of the needs of others, they will pay you for meeting that need. Every product you buy is someone's *fruit*. Fruit meets your needs, and you spend money to have it. That is the secret to prosperity. No fruit, no money.

Just having fruit will not bring you money. There are other steps involved before you can make any money from your fruit. I will explain that below. For now, just stop and say, "Father, thank You for making me fruitful in my spirit, soul, and body."

The Bible talks about different kinds of fruits that we need to produce.

FRUIT OF OUR BODY

The children we give birth to are the fruit of our body. We also labor or do work with our body that produces fruit. This is called the fruit of the land. If we do not work, there will not be any fruit.

> He will also bless the *fruit* of your womb and the *fruit* of your land (Deuteronomy 7:13).

> When you have gathered in the *fruit* of your labors from the field (Exodus 23:16).

> Give her of the *fruit* of her hands, and let her own works praise her in the gates (Proverbs 31:31).

THE PROCESS OF TAKING AND EXERCISING DOMINION

> Blessed shall be the *fruit* of your body (Deuteronomy 28:4).

FRUIT OF OUR LIPS: OUR WORDS

The words we speak are seeds. They will bring a harvest into our lives sooner or later. Our prosperity and health depend on the words of our mouth. The Bible says life and death are in the power of the tongue.

> A man will be satisfied with good by the *fruit* of his mouth (Proverbs 12:14).

> A man's stomach shall be satisfied from the *fruit* of his mouth; from the produce of his lips he shall be filled (Proverbs 18:20).

> I create the *fruit* of the lips (Isaiah 57:19).

FRUIT OF OUR MIND AND SOUL

Your prosperity depends on the fruit of your mind and spirit, not necessarily the fruit of your body (children). The soul is comprised of imagination, emotions, intellect, will, and memory. The fruit of our mind is our imagination. Every product and invention on earth are the fruit of someone's imagination (or mind). Some minds do not produce anything good because their imagination is constantly evil. We need to train our mind to think good thoughts because every thought has the potential to produce fruit—good or evil. Every good and evil deed we did began as an imagination or a thought in our mind.

God put the picture of our future in our mind. I call it a vision. The mind is not evil, and all imaginations are not evil. *Our mind is a blessing from God*, if we use it for the right cause. Our mind is God's manufacturing plant on earth to release new products and inventions. When He wants to release something new, He releases an idea to someone's mind or spirit. The fruit of the mind includes ideas, books, songs, drawings, specific knowledge, creativity, inventions, speech, and more. Anything we can use our imagination to do, build, or work is a fruit of our mind. The Bible says we have the mind of Christ *(1 Corinthians 2:16)*. We should be the most productive people on earth.

The wealthiest people on earth are those who use their minds. If you look at their lives, they may not necessarily be working hard with their bodies, but they are putting their minds to work. Your wealth is in the fruit of your mind. The more you put your mind to work, the more productive you become, and hence, the more prosperous you become.

> Commit your works to the Lord, and your *thoughts* will be established (Proverbs 16:3).

> The *plans* of the diligent lead surely to plenty (Proverbs 21:5).

> The *fruit* of their thoughts (Jeremiah 6:19).

FRUIT OF THE SPIRIT

Our spirit can produce fruit, too. We are familiar with the fruit of the spirit (love, joy, peace, and more) outlined in the Bible. We also need to bear a different kind of spiritual fruit—souls. When you bring a person to Christ, they are the fruit of your spirit; souls that we bring into the kingdom are called our spiritual children. The more spiritual children you have, the more you will be blessed.

> But the *fruit* of the Spirit is love, joy, peace… (Galatians 5:22).

The fruit of the spirit can also be made manifest through an idea, speech, books, songs, or messages God births in our hearts to share with others. They all have to come through our mind and body to benefit other people.

FINANCIAL FRUIT

When we sow a financial seed, it produces a harvest. It is also called fruit.

> Not that I seek the gift, but I seek the *fruit* that abounds to your account (Philippians 4:17).

GOD WANTS US TO BE FRUITFUL IN EVERYTHING

> You did not choose Me, but I chose you and appointed you that you should go and bear *fruit*, and that your *fruit* should remain, that whatever you ask the Father in My name He may give you (John 15:16).

> That you may walk worthy of the Lord, fully pleasing Him, being *fruitful* in every good work and increasing in the knowledge of God (Colossians 1:10).

When we recognize the seed God planted in our spirit, soul, and body and begin to produce fruit, we need to move into the next step, which is multiplication.

MULTIPLICATION

The next thing God told man to do was to multiply. After we produce fruit, we need to multiply that fruit. This means we need to find a way to mass-produce it. I am not talking about children here. I am talking about the fruit of your mind and spirit. When a person invents a product, he or she goes to a manufacturing company and asks them to reproduce it. The Hebrew word used for *multiply* is *rabah*, which means to be or become great, be or become many, be or become much, be or become numerous (of people, animals, or things), to make large, make many, enlarge.14 When you have an idea, song, book, or anything God put in your spirit or mind, you need to design it and find a way to multiply it. After you multiply, we move to the next stage.

FILL THE EARTH

To fill the earth means to distribute or market what God gave you. Many of us do not prosper because we do not have an idea or a product. Some of us do not know how to turn an idea into a product or a service. Others have a product but do not know how to distribute it. The more you distribute, the more you prosper.

The Hebrew word for fill the earth is *male*, which means to fill, be full, fullness, abundance, be accomplished.15 The people in the world are smarter about doing this than believers in the church. You need to fill the earth with your product. Companies spend billions of dollars to advertise or market their products. It does not matter how valuable or beneficial a product is; if you do not advertise it, no one will know about it, and the result will be that you will not prosper.

Companies like Coke, Pepsi, McDonald's, and Microsoft filled the earth with their products. They are some of the richest companies in the world. Once you fill the earth, then you move into the next stage.

SUBDUE

Once you distribute your product, then you take control of that one area you are focusing on with your product. Bill Gates subdued the area of computer technology and software for a long time all over the

---

14 James Strong, "7235. Rabah," Biblehub.com, accessed January 05, 2019, https://biblehub.com/hebrew/7235.htm.

15 James Strong, "4390. Male," Biblehub.com, accessed January 05, 2019, https://biblehub.com/hebrew/4390.htm.

world. Subdue means to take authority over something. Do it like no one has ever done it before. The Hebrew word for *subdue* is *kabash*, which means to subject, subdue, force, keep under, bring into bondage, make subservient.[16]

To subdue something, you need power and authority. Your product gives you power and authority to subdue that area. When you subdue, you will have dominion over it, and that is the next step.

DOMINION

Dominion is the ultimate purpose of God for man. Most people know in their heart they are created to rule and have dominion. Since the fall, when man lost his dominion, people no longer understood the process of dominion, and began to dominate each other. A person who does not have dominion over an area of life through their purpose and product will always try to dominate or control their fellow human beings with force instead because they feel insecure and left out of the crowd. Others may use their money and power to dominate. We were not created to rule over people.

The Hebrew word for dominion is *radah*, which means to rule, have dominion, dominate, tread down.[17] From Genesis to Revelation, it is God's plan that man have dominion. God is a king, and we are His children. What kings do is rule over a territory, which is called their kingdom.

If we study any successful business, person or endeavor we will find out that they followed these steps mentioned in the first chapter

---

16 James Strong, "3533. Kabash," Biblehub.com, accessed January 05, 2019, https://biblehub.com/hebrew/3533.htm.

17 James Strong, "7287. Radah," Biblehub.com, accessed January 05, 2019, https://biblehub.com/hebrew/7287.htm.

of Genesis. We didn't understand what it meant until now. These are the keys of the kingdom of God.

Adam was a king. Since the fall, God added another level of ministry to us: the ministry of priesthood. It is only for a period of time. At the end (after the redemption of creation), there will be only kings, just as it was in the beginning. That is why whenever God mentioned the position of man, He always put the kingship or royalty first and not the priesthood.

Right now, everyone in the body of Christ is a king and priest at the same time. In some circles, they divide the body into two, saying people who are in ministry are priests and others are kings. They do that because of the distinction we see in the Old Testament between priests and kings. David was a king, but he also had the anointing of a priest and prophet. Samuel is another example of this; he was a judge, priest, and a prophet.

When God brought the people of Israel out of Egypt, He said He wanted them to be a kingdom of priests.

> "And you shall be to Me a *kingdom of priests* and a holy nation." These are the words which you shall speak to the children of Israel (Exodus 19:6).

We see the same thing in New Testament.

> But you are a chosen generation, a *royal priesthood*, a holy nation, His own special people, that you may proclaim the praises of Him who called you out of darkness into His marvelous light (1 Peter 2:9).

> And from Jesus Christ, the faithful witness, the firstborn from the dead, and the ruler over the kings of the earth. To Him who loved us and washed us from our sins in His

THE PROCESS OF TAKING AND EXERCISING DOMINION

own blood, and has *made us kings and priests* to His God and Father, to Him be glory and dominion forever and ever. Amen (Revelation 1:5-6).

And have *made us kings and priests* to our God; and we shall reign on the earth (Revelation 5:10).

There will never be night again. They will not need the light of a lamp or the light of the sun, because the Lord God will give them light. And they will rule as *kings* forever and ever (Revelation 22:5, NCV).

None of these verses say God made some kings and others priests. Instead, they say He made us kings and priests. That includes everyone. In Revelation 22 mentions only kings. Amen to that!

CHAPTER 12

THE PURPOSE, POWER, AND FUNCTION OF ISRAEL

There are three sets of Scriptures that are very important for us to understand the entire Bible and God's plan for earth and mankind. The first one is Genesis 1:26-28, the second is Genesis 12:2–3, and the third is Matthew 16:18–19. The entire purpose and plan of God hangs on those three groups of verses.

We have touched on Genesis 1:26-28. Now we are going to deal with the other two groups. The second one is in Genesis 12:2–3. Those two verses in Genesis 12 contain the blueprint for founding the nation of Israel.

> I will make you a great nation; I will bless you, and make your name great; and you shall be a blessing. I will bless those who bless you, and I will curse him who curses you; and in you all the families of the earth shall be blessed (Genesis 12:2-3).

These verses are part of Abraham's call and God's promises to him. God wanted to make Abraham a great nation. Why would God want a nation? Those verses reveal the purpose, power, and function of the nation of Israel. God wants to bless the entire planet through them, all the families of the earth, in every nation. If anyone blesses them, God will bless them, and if anyone curses them, God will curse them. That is dominion!

When we study the Bible, we realize that God has the same plan for Adam (mankind), the nation of Israel, and the church (also a nation to God). He did not introduce anything new. God's purpose and plans are the same in every generation. Their functions were a little different, but His purpose and principles remained the same. How were the functions different? The way Adam functioned in the garden is the way Israel functioned as a nation, and the way the Israel functioned is the way the church was supposed to function: as a nation.

The church is not a political nation. It's a spiritual nation within a political nation. Israel was a political and spiritual nation at the same time with specific physical boundaries. The church, as a spiritual nation, does not have any physical boundaries. Our jurisdiction surpasses any physical boundaries, and includes the entire planet.

The purpose of the three entities are the same—to establish God's kingdom and will. If that is not happening, everything we do is a waste of time and energy.

God had blessed Israel and placed them above every other nation to be the light and blessing to the whole world.

> Also today the Lord has proclaimed you to be His special people, just as He promised you, that you should keep all His commandments, and that He will set you high above all nations which He has made, in praise, in name, and in honor, and that you may be a holy people to the Lord your God, just as He has spoken (Deuteronomy 26:18–19).

God's plan originally started with one man, then expanded to a nation, and then finally a governing body called the church within every nation. Local churches are supposed to function like a self-governing kingdom community in every city and town, then infiltrate the entire city or town for Jesus and His kingdom. Jesus taught this concept in the kingdom parables of the leaven and the mustard seed. They start very small, but when they reach completion, they engulf everything around them.

The Great Commission Jesus commanded in Matthew 28 had to do with discipling nations. To disciple a nation, we need to be above every nation in praise, in name, and in honor, as Deuteronomy says. Otherwise, we cannot disciple any nation. The reason the church is not able to disciple any nation, and we are only qualified to evangelize, is because we do not have the honor, influence, and position to get the job done.

In most places, the best we do is conduct a crusade, organize street evangelism, and distribute free food. Jesus did not come to train His disciples on how to conduct the best crusade; He came to train them to establish His kingdom.

In most places, the church is considered a vile thing because it is operating only as a religion or as a religious entity, looking for something free from people and government. They have no name or honor. This will only change when believers are taught to recognize their purpose and are trained to walk in their calling by identifying and developing their gifts. Once a church recognizes its purpose, nothing will stop it, and things will begin to turn around.

If you study the scriptures, you will notice that both Israel and the church have the same function and purpose. Whatever God told Israel, He told the church as well.

Below are a few examples.

DISCOVERING PURPOSE, CALLING AND GIFTS

Isreal	The Church
When God called Abraham, He promised him that He would bless all the nations of the earth through him *(Genesis 22:18)*	Jesus told the church to go and disciple all nations He used a different word, but it had the same meaning *(Matthew 28:19)* You cannot disciple a nation without being a blessing to them
God promised Abraham that his descendants would possess the gates of their enemies *(Genesis 22:17)*	Jesus said He will build His church and the gates of hell would not prevail against it *(Matthew 16:18)*
God promised Abraham land *(Genesis 12:1–7)*	Jesus promised that we would inherit the earth *(Matthew 5:5)*
God promised Abraham that He would start a nation through him *(Genesis 12:1–7)*	We are called a nation and Jesus told us to go and disciple all nations *(Matthew 21:43; 28:18–20; 1 Peter 2:9)*
Israel is called the children of God *(Exodus 4:22; Deuteronomy 14:1)*	Anyone who believes in Jesus Christ is also called a child of God *(John 1:12)*
God wanted them to be the head and above every other nation *(Deuteronomy 28:13)*	We are called the light of this world and the salt of the earth *(Matthew 5:13–14)*
God wanted them to be a kingdom of priests and a holy nation *(Exodus 19:6)*	The church is called a royal priesthood and a holy nation *(1 Peter 2:9)*
God named Jacob, his children, and the nation, Israel	The church is called the Israel of God *(Galatians 6:16)*
God used twelve men *(sons of Jacob)* to establish the nation of Israel	Jesus used twelve apostles as the foundation of His church *(Ephesians 2:20)*
God wanted Israel to make known that He is their God to the ends of the earth *(Joshua 4:23–24; Psalm 59:13, 98:3)*	Jesus told the church to go to the ends of the earth *(Acts 1:8)*

THE PURPOSE, POWER, AND FUNCTION OF ISRAEL

Isreal	The Church
God promised the land of Canaan to the people of Israel *(Genesis 15:18)*	Jesus promised and gave the jurisdiction of the entire earth to the church *(Matthew 5:5, 16:19)*
Israel is called a nation	The church is called a nation *(Matthew 21:43; 1 Peter 2:9)*
They were called the church, or congregation, in the wilderness *(Acts 7:38 KJV; Exodus 12:3)*	We are the church in the New Testament
All of the inhabitants of the land were afraid and became fainthearted because of them *(Exodus 23:27; Joshua 2:10)*	Fear came upon every soul because of the church and what the Lord did through them *(Acts 2:43)*
God told Moses to appoint judges and officers all throughout the land to administer justice to the people *(Deuteronomy 16:18)*	Jesus and Paul told us to do the same in the church, to appoint elders *(Matthew 18:15–17; Acts 14:23; 1 Corinthians 6:1–5; Titus 1:5)*

Don't ever let anyone convince you that God didn't bless you with the same blessing He blessed the Jews.

- You are a child of God (John 1:12).

- You are a seed of Abraham (Galatians 3:29).

- You are a chosen generation (1 Peter 2:9).

- You received the promise of Abraham (Galatians 3:14).

- You are a co-heir with Christ (Romans 8:17).

DISCOVERING PURPOSE, CALLING AND GIFTS

You are grafted into the same blessings and promises God gave to the Jews.

Actually, you and I received a better covenant than the Old Testament covenant. This is not a replacement theology; this is called extended theology or oneness theology. God decided to extend the same blessings, promises, favor, protection, and prosperity He gave to the Jews, to the Gentiles through Jesus Christ, and create "one new man" *(Ephesians 2:14–22)*.

Don't ever let anyone deceive you by saying you have to take part in a Jewish ritual to receive a special blessing from your own Father. We need to pray for the peace of Jerusalem and for the salvation of the Jewish people, but we do not need to come under the Law of Moses or any particular culture. The New Testament makes that clear.

God sent His Son to die for our sins and reinstate His kingdom purpose. He instituted the church, comprised of both Jews and Gentiles, to represent Him and His kingdom. This is not a new revelation I just discovered. The revelation of God's kingdom is as old as the heavens and the earth. You can find it in Genesis and all through the Bible.

THE PURPOSE AND FUNCTION OF ISRAEL CHART

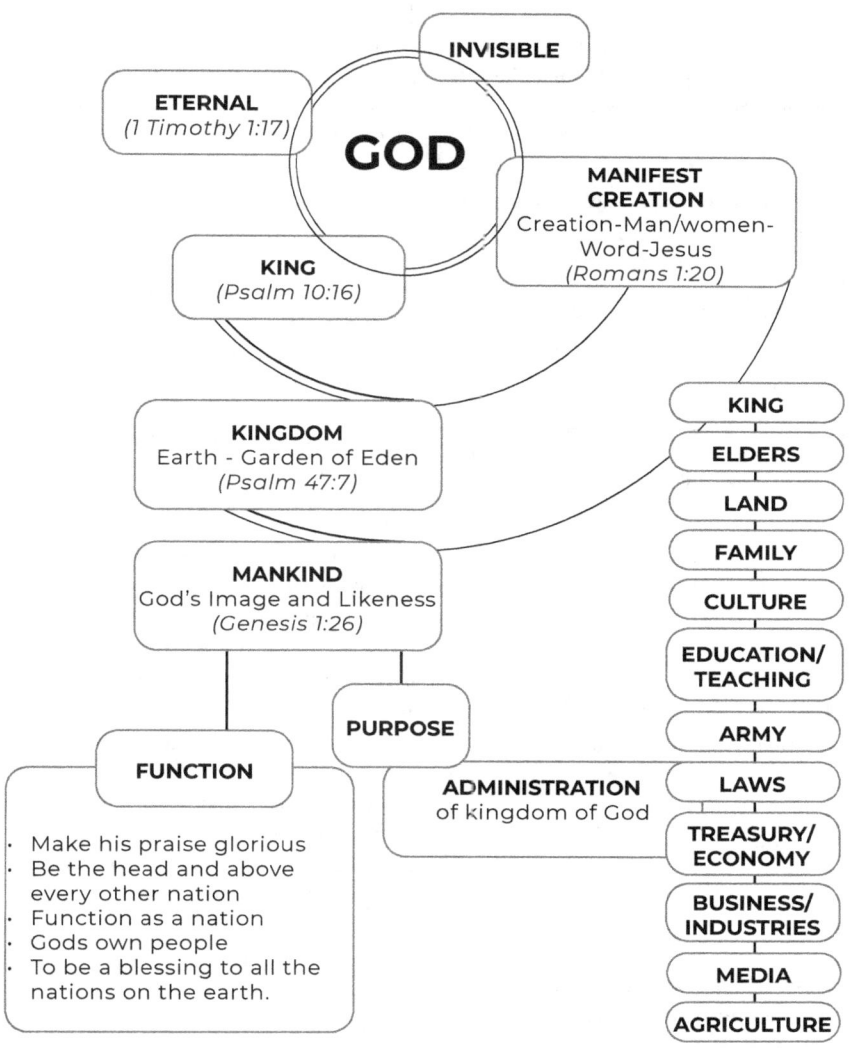

DISCOVERING PURPOSE, CALLING AND GIFTS

Below are some more comparisons between mankind, Israel, and the church.

Isreal	The Church
God wanted to be their King and Ruler, but they wanted kings like other nations *(1 Samuel 8:4–7)*	Jesus wanted to be the only Shepherd of the church, but we have millions of shepherds that divide the body into pieces for their own personal benefit *(John 10:11; Hebrews 13:20)*
The nation of Israel had an economy *(Deuteronomy 8:17–18)*	The church had an economy of its own *(Acts 2:44–45)*
The nation of Israel had a judicial system *(Deuteronomy 16:18)*	The church is supposed to judge and solve their own problems *(1 Corinthians 6:1–7)*
The nation of Israel had elders that were appointed in every city and stood in the gates *(Numbers 11:16–17)*	The church was run by elders in the first century *(Acts 14:23; Titus 1:5)*
Israel was the head and above every other nation *(Deuteronomy 28:1)*	The church is supposed to be the head and above every other nation. This means that believers are supposed to be the most productive people in every nation. For this to happen, we need an entirely different training system than we have right now. The system we have right now is not geared toward preparing an individual to become productive or excel in any area; instead, it is geared toward escaping from this planet
Israel had an agricultural and food production system *(Leviticus 19:23)*	The church needs to have its own agricultural and food production system

THE PURPOSE, POWER, AND FUNCTION OF ISRAEL

Isreal	The Church
Israel had its own educational system, which was different from other nations *(Deuteronomy 4:9–10)*	The church needs its own educational system, which trains people based on their purpose, calling, and gifts *(Matthew 28:20)*
God was watching over Israel day and night *(Psalm 121:4)*	Jesus said He would never leave nor forsake us *(Hebrews 13:5b)*
Adam was the firstborn of all mankind. Israel is the firstborn of God *(Exodus 4:22)*	Church is called the firstborn of God and the firstborn of many brethren *(Hebrews 12:23)*
Adam's responsibility was to keep the gates of hell from operating on the earth *(Genesis 2:15)*	Jesus said the church would destroy the works of the gates of hell *(Matthew 16:18)*
God promised Abraham that his seed should possess the gates of his enemies *(Genesis 22:17)*	
We are the seed of Abraham by faith in Christ *(Galatians 3:29)*	Jesus is the Seed God promised to Abraham *(Galatians 3:16)*
Israel is the seed of Abraham	The church is the seed of Abraham *(Romans 4:11–17)*. We are grafted into the same vine *(Romans 11:17)*. This means we share the same life and the same promises. What Israel had is now ours through Christ Jesus too
God began with the act of creation in Genesis *(Genesis 1:1–28)*	Jesus began with an act of creation at a wedding in Cana *(John 2:6–8)*
God told man to have dominion over the fish of the seas first *(Genesis 1:26)*	Jesus started dominion over fish by giving a miraculous catch of fish to Peter and Andrew *(Luke 5:4–9)*

DISCOVERING PURPOSE, CALLING AND GIFTS

ONE IN CHRIST

First of all, the Law (Old Covenant) was given to the children of Israel—the Jews, not the Gentiles. A Gentile has nothing to do with the covenant God made with the Israelites. To the Jews and God, we were called, uncircumcised, and were "without Christ, being aliens from the commonwealth of Israel and strangers from the covenants of promise, having no hope, and without God in the world" *(Ephesians 2:12)*. This was our spiritual and social status before Christ came, so putting a Jewish prayer shawl on your head will not make you any more spiritual, neither will it make you a Jew. Living in a barn won't make you a cow!

Many are trying to become Jews these days by putting on prayer shawls, keeping the Shabbat and reciting Hebrew prayers, blowing the shofar, or sticking something on the doorpost of their house. (I hope they are not getting circumcised too, as circumcision is the first requirement to adhere to the Law and become Jewish.) Those who expected new believers to do this in the first-century church were called Judaizers. They still exist today.

I know people who call themselves Christians but have officially converted to Judaism. Just because you keep a bunch of rules doesn't make you a Jew. Please don't misunderstand me. I am not anti-Semitic. I love the people of Israel and pray for their salvation. Listen to what Paul writes.

> For he is not a Jew who is one outwardly, nor is circumcision that which is outward in the flesh; but he is a Jew who is one inwardly; and circumcision is that of the heart, in the Spirit, not in the letter; whose praise is not from men but from God (Romans 2:28–29).
>
> Who are Israelites, to whom pertain the adoption, the glory, the covenants, the giving of the law, the service of God,

THE PURPOSE, POWER, AND FUNCTION OF ISRAEL

> and the promises; of whom are the fathers and from whom, according to *the flesh, Christ came*, who is over all, the eternally blessed God. Amen. But it is not that the word of God has taken no effect. For they are not all Israel who are of Israel (Romans 9:4–6).

This says that according to the flesh, Christ came through the people of Israel. But no longer do we know Christ after the flesh. Once He died and rose again, He was no longer a Jewish carpenter. He is now King of Kings and Lord of Lords, the King of the whole earth.

> And He died for all, that those who live should live no longer for themselves, but for Him who died for them and rose again. Therefore, from now on, we regard *no one* according to the flesh. Even though we have known Christ according to the flesh, yet now we know Him thus no longer (2 Corinthians 5:15–16).

Other people say we need to discover our Jewish roots to receive our blessings, but really, we need to be rooted and grounded in love. That is the biggest problem in church today; very few are rooted in the love of God. Instead, we are rooted in some sect, culture, religion, or ideology. We should be free in Jesus's name. Please pray the prayer Paul prayed in Ephesians. He did not pray we should be rooted and grounded in our Jewish roots. He prayed this:

> For this reason I bow my knees to the Father of our Lord Jesus Christ, from whom the whole family in heaven and earth is named, that He would grant you,
>
> according to the riches of His glory, to be strengthened with might through His Spirit in the inner man, that Christ may dwell in your hearts through faith; that you, being rooted and grounded in love, may be able to comprehend with

DISCOVERING PURPOSE, CALLING AND GIFTS

all the saints what is the width and length and depth and height—to know the love of Christ which passes knowledge; that you may be filled with all the fullness of God. Now to Him who is able to do exceedingly abundantly above all that we ask or think, according to the power that works in us, to Him be glory in the church by Christ Jesus to all generations, forever and ever. Amen *(Ephesians 3:14–21)*.

CHAPTER 13
THE PURPOSE, POWER, AND FUNCTION OF THE CHURCH

As we read before, everything God created has a specific purpose and function. If we do not understand the difference between them, our lives will be out of balance and ineffective. Many confuse function with purpose and vice versa. Just because something is functioning does not mean it is fulfilling its purpose.

The purpose of the sun is to rule over the day and give light and heat to our planet. The way it functions is through the chemical reactions that occur inside the sun to produce heat and light; these help it fulfill its purpose.

The purpose of an apple tree is to produce apples. It has a trunk, branches, and roots to help produce apples. Think about other examples. Make a list of each, their specific purpose and function, and meditate on them.

THE PURPOSE AND POWER OF THE CHURCH

There has been a massive exodus of people from the mainline churches. They are tired of doing the same thing over and over again and expecting

DISCOVERING PURPOSE, CALLING AND GIFTS

a different result. This exodus might be the biggest in size so far and might be much larger in number than the one from Egypt.

People are looking for something authentic. Their spirit is longing for something real. They know they have been created for something different, and it's not what they have been doing. Many try to "shrink" the church and meet in small groups in homes, thinking this will meet their need.

As a result, there has been a large "house church" movement in almost every country. Most of these groups come together and do exactly what they did in the church they left, only on a smaller scale. They eat and drink coffee and donuts, but they are not effective because they are not fulfilling their purpose. These changes are focused on tweaking the function of the church rather than rediscovering and fulfilling its purpose.

Very few understand the purpose of the church in the same way that only a few understand the purpose of mankind. When you bring together a group of people who do not understand their purpose, it doesn't matter what they try to do; it will not produce the fruit they expect. That is why this book is focusing on first reestablishing the purpose of man. Until we do that, nothing else will work in our society.

Nothing will work as it is supposed to work because we are missing the foundation. This applies to family life, government, church, economy, education, and anything else you can imagine. *What can you build that will last if the very foundation is missing?* We have been laboring in vain, trying to catch the wind. At the end of the day, look at what you have accomplished. Was any of it meaningful? We need to ask this question. Many are frustrated about their lives and what has happened to them. It's too late to go back and fix anything in the past, but we can focus on the next generation and help them make improvements; we do not want to pass on what does not work. Let's rebuild the foundation so it is stable and secure instead.

Shrinking the church or starting a house church won't solve the current church dilemma. That's like taking the same gift and putting new wrapping paper around it. As the old saying goes, it's like putting a bandage on a tumor. The tumor has to be rooted out.

The demonic world had access to our planet prior to man's fall. That is why they came into the garden, but they did not have any authority or right to rule our planet. Adam had the key, and he could have let them in or kept them out from receiving the right to rule. Through deception, they stole the right from Adam and Eve.

God told Adam to have dominion over the earth. The reason God told Adam to rule this planet or the garden of Eden was to keep Satan and his demons out of that kind of position. God did not want them to get a foothold anywhere on earth. It was man's responsibility to protect this earth from the enemy. As we know, Adam failed in his assignment and gave the enemy the right to operate here.

The devil built his kingdom using man and the earthly resources that belonged to Adam. Jesus, the last Adam, came to defeat the enemy and crushed the head of the serpent as prophesied in Genesis 3. Jesus restored all authority in heaven and on earth. He judged the world and the ruler of it *(John 12:31, 16:11)*.

Once again, God wanted to give dominion to mankind as He did in the beginning. He gave the kingdom and keys back to mankind in the form of the church. I would like to show you the parallel between what God told Adam and what Jesus taught about the church. This is one of the most powerful revelations God has ever given me.

As we learned, Genesis 1:26 is the key verse to understanding our purpose and function: "Then God said, 'Let Us make man in Our

DISCOVERING PURPOSE, CALLING AND GIFTS

image, according to Our likeness; let them have dominion over the fish of the sea, over the birds of the air, and over the cattle, over all the earth and over every creeping thing that creeps on the earth'" *(Genesis 1:26)*.

This verse says God created us in His image and likeness and said, "Let them have dominion." As already mentioned, we need to notice that God did not include Himself in the process of dominion, only in the process of creating us. He gave total freedom to mankind to do nearly whatever they wanted on and with the earth. They could save or destroy this planet. They could depend or work independently of Him.

Jesus said the same thing about the church when He spoke about its purpose and function in Matthew 16:18–19.

> And I also say to you that you are Peter, and on this rock I will build My church, and the gates of Hades shall not prevail against it. And I will give you the keys of the kingdom of heaven, and whatever you bind on earth will be bound in heaven, and whatever you loose on earth will be loosed in heaven (Matthew 16:18–19).

Just as God was involved in the act of our creation but not involved in exercising dominion, Jesus started the church, and said, "I will build My church and the gates of hell will not prevail against it." He is the One building it, and He made it very clear why He was building it. He did it so the gates of hell would not have free reign on earth, but He did not include Himself in exercising the church's authority.

The purpose of the church is to keep the enemy from exercising dominion on earth, just like Adam was supposed to keep the demonic forces out of the garden. When it came to exercising dominion, Jesus did not involve Himself. He said, "I will give you [the church] the keys of the kingdom and whatever you bind [forbid] on earth will be bound [forbidden] in heaven and whatever you loose [permit] will be loosed [permitted] in heaven or by heaven" *(Matthew 16:19)*. That is exercising dominion. Notice that it is *us* that does the binding and loosing, not Jesus. He did not include Himself in that process, in the same way God did not in Genesis.

You may wonder where I came up with the above phrases added in brackets for Matthew 16:19. I received it from the Bible itself. Please read that verse in the following translations:

> And I will give you the keys of the Kingdom of Heaven. Whatever you forbid on earth will be forbidden in heaven, and whatever you permit on earth will be permitted in heaven (NLT).

> I will give you the keys of the kingdom of heaven; the things you don't allow on earth will be the things that God does not allow, and the things you allow on earth will be the things that God allows (NCV).

The religious spirit taught us that this verse is talking about binding and loosing demons. The church has been binding demons for almost two thousand years, and still, there is no lack of them around us. If you study the New Testament, you will see that Jesus and His apostles never bound a demon; they always cast them out. That is what Jesus told us to do.

Jesus gave the church absolute authority to decide what happened on earth in the same way that He gave it to Adam. Do you see the parallel between the creation of Adam and his purpose and the building of the church and its purpose? The church is in a terrible state today. We have turned the church into a religious organization, a social club, or a stage for musical productions. How horrible is that?

Today it is the church's choice to allow or not allow anything they want or do not want. We have the total authority given by our King

DISCOVERING PURPOSE, CALLING AND GIFTS

Jesus to exercise jurisdiction over this entire planet, just like Adam had in Genesis before the fall.

Understanding this similarity between the account of the creation of mankind and the building of the church by Jesus Christ was revolutionary for me. Both were created or established for the same purpose and have the same power.

The same way Adam had the authority to give or deny the right to the demonic world to set up their kingdom on earth, the church has the authority to deny or give the right to the demonic world from operating on the earth. It is a simple but very profound truth.

Adam failed to exercise his authority, and the church has done the same, allowing all kinds of evil without realizing who is allowing it. The majority of the church world blames the devil for what is happening here, without knowing they are the ones giving the devil permission. They are the ones that hold the keys of God's kingdom. The devil doesn't own any keys.

The moment the church wakes up and becomes what she was intended to be and functions the way she was intended to function from the beginning, this world will be a totally different place. The church's primary purpose is to deny the gates of hell the ability to operate on the earth. We should not be giving any right to the demonic world to accomplish any of their agenda on earth.

Just as mankind has purpose and function, the church also has purpose and function. Just as the majority of mankind is functioning but are not fulfilling their purpose, the majority of the church is functioning but are not fulfilling their purpose. The same problems mankind has will be manifested in the church because the church is made of people.

We spend millions of dollars on the function of the church, on music, on lights, on buildings, and on technologies to keep people entertained. I wish we spent a fraction of that money on training people to rediscover and fulfill their purpose. This world would be a better place in just ten years.

Most of the church is overtaken by the religious spirit or the spirit of this world. Because of this, there is little difference between Christianity or any other religion. We think we don't worship idols or superheroes. Believe me, the church is full of them. Your priority is your idol. Whatever you spend the majority of your time on, other than God and building His kingdom, is your idol. Whatever you draw your joy and fulfillment from is your idol. Just take a survey of your life and see where God is in your life and who or what else is sitting on the throne of your heart.

The tragic truth is that people will read something like this and get up and go on as if nothing is wrong, or they did not understand what they just read. They will go and buy the next season ticket for their favorite sport team or something similar. The strongholds of the enemy are too deep for us to even recognize there is something wrong with the way we do things.

DESTROYING THE OPERATION OF THE GATES OF HELL

This is the main purpose of the church. This has to be done on two levels, both in the spiritual and in the natural. As I mentioned before, first, we need to identify the gates of hell in our community, state, or nation. Then we must receive guidance and wisdom from the Holy Spirit on how to confront them. The way the Holy Spirit directs us to confront a gate will be different each time. There is no one tool fit for all systems in the kingdom.

Our ultimate goal is to bring all of Jesus' enemies to His footstool. That is what He is waiting for. We are on a joint mission with the Father to accomplish that goal.

MORE ON THE POWER OF THE CHURCH

Be a gate of heaven on earth over the natural and spirit world. Since a gate is something that gives or denies access, churches hold the authority to give or deny access to anything that happens here. We are supposed to function as the gate of heaven and forbid the gate of hell from operating.

We hold the keys of God's kingdom. The person who holds the key has the right to permit or not permit someone from going in or coming out. Imagine that the Queen of England has given you all the keys to all of her palaces and their rooms. Even if she has to open or go into some rooms, she needs your permission to allow her to go in now. This is an analogy of Jesus and the church.

Jesus gave the keys of His kingdom to us. Imagine how much He trusted us. We have been walking around with them and do not know how to use them. If the president of a country sent their troops to a battlefield, they have the authorization from the government to confront the enemy and do what is required of them.

They do not need to call the president every time before they use their weapons. That is what we do. We tell Jesus to do everything that we're supposed to be doing. He gave us the authorization and the keys. Now if He needs to do something, He has to do it with us and through us. That is a powerful truth. May God grant us wisdom to understand it today!

Most of the time when people pray, they are asking Jesus to do something they are already authorized to accomplish. It would be like an army calling the leader of their country and asking them to do what they're supposed to be doing. The leader is not in the battlefield. They can't fire the weapon. The soldiers have to do it. It is same with us. We have not been trained this way. We have been trained to be spectators and watch someone do something on a platform on a Sunday morning. *This has to change.*

The whole purpose of ministers is to equip the members of the church to do the work of the ministry. If they are not doing that, they are building their own kingdoms.

That is why Jesus said, "What we bind on earth will be bound in heaven and whatever we loose on earth will be loosed in heaven." That means that whatever we authorize on earth, heaven will authorize. Both actions are done on earth; heaven responds to our actions.

Now let us explore some of the functions of the church. I won't be able to mention every function, but I am happy to cover the most important ones.

THE FUNCTIONS OF THE CHURCH

Functions are intended to help us fulfill our purpose. The same way the function of the church is to help her fulfill her purpose. How do we stop the gates of hell from fulfilling their assignment? Jesus told us clearly.

ADMINISTERING THE KINGDOM OF GOD

As we learned in the other volumes of the *Kingdom Secrets* series, the church should function as a governing body of the kingdom of God. Jesus came to give us a kingdom and our duty is to administer it. He needed a body of people to do that; and for that purpose, He established His church. How do we administer the kingdom of God?

DISCIPLING NATIONS

> Go therefore and make disciples of all the nations, baptizing them in the name of the Father and of the Son and of the Holy Spirit, teaching them to observe all things that I have commanded you; and lo, I am with you always, even to the end of the age. Amen (Matthew 28:19–20).

Another major purpose of the church is to disciple individuals. They in turn will disciple their cities and nations. Discipleship begins by releasing people into their God-given destinies. Every time a person is released to fulfill their destiny, their destiny is connected to the destiny of a nation.

Note that in Matthew 28 Jesus did not say go and make disciples *from* every nation, but go and make disciples *of* all nations. We have been making disciples from nations for too long. We are entering a new season in which we are beginning to disciple nations, cities, and tribes for Jesus Christ. The Great Commission is not about evangelizing nations or people groups, but about discipling nations. I have dedicated the last chapter of this book to discipling nations.

SAVING THE WORLD

This might sound strange. Are we supposed to save the world? Yes. God sent His Son Jesus to save the world, not destroy it. We have been waiting for the end of the world.

> For God so loved the world that He gave His only begotten Son, that whoever believes in Him should not perish but have everlasting life. For God did not send His Son into the world to condemn the world, but that the world through Him might be saved (John 3:16–17).

THE PURPOSE, POWER, AND FUNCTION OF THE CHURCH

Most people are familiar with John 3:16; however, not very many know the next verse. God wants to save this world because it was created by Jesus and for Him. This says the same thing.

> And if anyone hears My words and does not believe, I do not judge him; for I did not come to judge the world but to save the world (John 12:47).

Jesus already judged the world and the god of it two thousand years ago. We are supposed to enforce that sentence upon the enemy kingdom, but we have been slacking off. Why should we enforce it? Because we are the ones who permitted the enemy to do what he does. The enemy is acting like nothing has changed. Unfortunately, he is behaving the same as before the death and resurrection of Jesus. That should never be the case.

If Jesus died and took away the sin of the whole world and defeated Satan and received all authority in heaven and on earth, what should have changed in your society and the life around you? If nothing has changed for the better, then why not?

> Now is the judgment of this world; now the ruler of this world will be cast out (John 12:31).

> And when He has come, He will convict the world of sin, and of righteousness, and of judgment: of sin, because they do not believe in Me; of righteousness, because I go to My Father and you see Me no more; of judgment, because the ruler of this world is judged (John 16:8–11).

The above events took place two thousand years ago. Why are we not enforcing the victory of Jesus upon the enemy kingdom? Because we are not equipped to do that. The majority of believers do not function in their purpose, calling, and gifts. They are waiting to fly away, singing, "This world is not my home." This must change.

GOING INTO ALL THE WORLD

> And He said to them, "Go into all the world and preach the gospel to every creature" (Mark 16:15).

In Matthew, Jesus told us to disciple nations, and in Mark, He gave us a clue on how to do it: by going *into* the world. To save the world, we need to go into all the world. How do we do this? What is the world? The word for *world* in Greek is *kosmos*, which means any orderly system on planet Earth.[18] Earth is the physical planet, and the world is the system by which the Earth operates. Without the world, the planet cannot function and it will remain barren.

Jesus commanded us to go into the world. There is an economic world, a political world, a media-based world, an educational world, a natural world, a fashion-focused world, a technological world, and so on. We are supposed to train believers and release them to infiltrate all these different systems for kingdom purposes.

We have been going *around* the world instead of going *into* the world. The whole purpose of the Kingdom School is to equip the body of Christ to go into the world and make disciples of all nations.

PREACHING THE GOSPEL TO EVERY CREATURE

The fall of man affected the entire creation. Jesus came to redeem and restore what was brought under corruption. He did His part and left the rest of the job for us. He paid the price of redemption. The blood of Jesus is sufficient and powerful enough to save and redeem everything that was lost. In order for that to happen, we need to preach the gospel

---

18 James Strong, "2889. Kosmos," Biblehub.com, accessed January 19, 2019, https://biblehub.com/greek/2889.htm.

to every creature, and not just humans. That is what Paul did during his ministry days *(Colossians 1:23)*.

ENFORCING JESUS' VICTORY OVER THE ENEMY: JUDGMENT IS ALREADY DONE!

The church needs to enforce the victory of the cross. This world, Satan, and sin have already been judged by Jesus. If we do not enforce the victory, the enemy will continue to act like nothing has changed. We are not here to bind Satan or demons. We are here to take back the ground they control and possess.

TEACHING THE WISDOM OF GOD TO PRINCIPALITIES AND POWERS

Ephesians 3:10 says the church is supposed to teach the manifold wisdom of God to the principalities and powers. Because of ignorance, many believers try to pull down principalities or even bind them. We are not supposed to do that. Do you really want to pull down principalities to the ground near you? Or close to where you are and live next to them? I don't think so. They have been left in the heavenlies for a reason. We are seated in Christ Jesus far above all principalities and powers *(Ephesians 1:20, 2:6)*.

SOLVING PROBLEMS FOR PEOPLE

Whether they are natural or spiritual problems, the church should have the solutions. When we solve problems for people and our community, it brings honor and credibility to God. Joseph solved the famine problem in Egypt. Jesus said when two people are having an unresolved issue, they should go to the church and solve it *(Matthew 18:15–17)*. Paul exhorted the church to solve their own problems, in both spiritual and legal matters *(1 Corinthians 6:1–7)*.

FUNCTIONING AS A NATION WITHIN A NATION, NOT AS A RELIGIOUS OR CHARITABLE INSTITUTION

> But you are a chosen generation, a royal priesthood, a holy nation, His own special people, that you may proclaim the praises of Him who called you out of darkness into His marvelous light (1 Peter 2:9).

Whatever a nation has, the church should have, as well. The only difference between us should be that our Head is Jesus Christ, not some worldly leader. We should have an economy, agriculture, culture, and an educational system that is different from the people around us. When people from the outside look at us, they should understand the difference and the peculiarity. In truth, they should envy the church and want to become part of it.

BEING THE SALT OF THE EARTH AND LIGHT OF THE WORLD

Salt preserves and sustains. Its primary function is to bring taste or make food edible. That is our function, too. We should preserve and sustain the earth and make life on earth tasteful. Most people out there are tired of their life and feel that it is meaningless. We bring purpose where there is none and hope where there is despair.

Light solves the problem of darkness. We are the light of this world and not the light of heaven. Darkness prevails when light is absent. The reason the works of darkness are prevailing in many places is because the light is absent. Our governments, schools, media, you name it: anywhere the light is absent, we will see darkness flourishing.

TEACHING, EQUIPPING, AND TRAINING

Jesus said to go and teach everything He commanded us *(Matthew 28:20)*. Then in Ephesians 4:11–12, we read about the purpose of the fivefold ministry and how gifts are to equip the saints to do the work of the ministry. Our ministers are supposed to train believers to discover their purpose, calling, and gifts, and then release them to function in their respective places.

In today's church world, we do not see this happening. The majority of the ministers want to keep people to themselves and use them to fulfill a vision they believe God gave them. They do not release people; as a result, people don't grow. They remain spiritual babies, used and abused by the leaders. They do not even know how to pray for a headache. Instead, they run to the medicine shelf looking for some pills.

How will we know if a minister is really called by God? They will have a heart to equip and release people to fulfill their calling instead of using them to build a personal empire. All these personal empires will crumble at the end of their own lifetimes. What if these ministers had trained and released people to build God's kingdom in their communities instead? That ministry would go on forever. Our world would be a different place by now.

WORSHIPPING

We have made this into singing and turned it into one of our main purposes. Most churches teach their people that God created them to worship Him by singing. They spend most of their time singing instead of equipping. What if we use the majority of our time training people about how to influence the world? The first-century church did not spend a majority of their time singing. They were focused on infiltrating their communities with the leaven of the kingdom.

Praise is only a function of the church, not its purpose. We should keep it in the place it belongs and not make it the reason for our existence.

BECOMING A DWELLING PLACE FOR GOD

When we come together as a local church, we are supposed to create a dwelling place for God. We are the temple of God and the Holy Spirit *(1 Corinthians 3:16, 6:19)*. Each of us is a living stone and plays an integral part in the Big Picture. We do not need to sing to create a dwelling place for God. In the New Testament, it's not our praises that are the dwelling place of God, but our bodies that are the dwelling place of God. That is a huge difference.

Most of the church world still operates in the Old Testament paradigm. Every time they gather, they try singing to create a dwelling place for God, without ever realizing God already dwells in them, and their bodies are His temple.

Most do not submit their bodies as a temple for God; instead, they treat it as an idol. They dress it, polish it, and are involved in self-worship. That is an abomination to God, and at the end of their lives, those same bodies become a curse to them instead of a blessing.

FUNCTIONING AS A FAMILY OR COMMUNITY

Another function of the church is to be a family or a community. Church is made of people, and people are from different families. But as a body, we form a bigger family. Each member of the family has a different function. As you know, every family has problems because people have problems. Problems don't annul family. We need to stay connected and work through our issues, thereby making the family of God stronger.

Because of individualism, people do not understand the value of family. They only tend to think about themselves. We need to lay aside our individualistic mindset and learn to think as a family and community.

PURPOSE AND FUNCTION OF THE CHURCH CHART

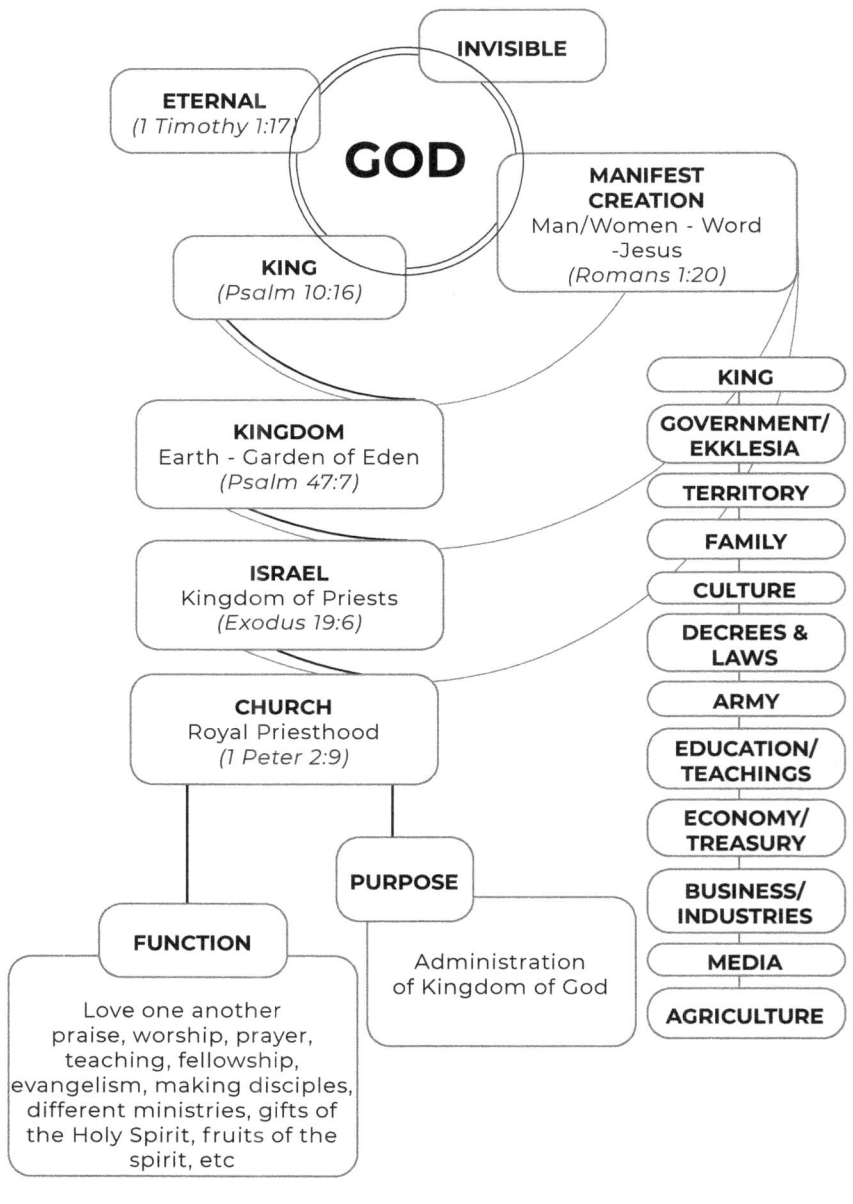

CHAPTER 14

CALLING –THE KEY TO FULFILLING YOUR PURPOSE

IF YOU ARE SAVED, THEN YOU ARE CALLED

To fulfill God's purpose for our lives when we are saved, each of us receives a calling to know which arena we're supposed to fill. God calls us according to His purpose and not ours *(Romans 8:28; 2 Timothy 1:9)*. There are different types of calling. Moses was called to be a deliverer; Peter was called to be an apostle; Joseph was called to be a prime minister. But everybody is called to fulfill the same purpose, which is to have dominion over the earth on some level.

GOD CALLS US ACCORDING TO HIS PURPOSE

After we understand our purpose, the next step is to recognize our calling. Believe it or not, there is a specific call of God on your life. *Calling is an act of God to release you to fulfill your destiny or purpose.*

God calls us according to His purpose, which He purposed in Christ Jesus before the world began. The Bible clearly relates our calling with God's purpose.

DISCOVERING PURPOSE, CALLING AND GIFTS

> And we know that all things work together for good to those who love God, to those who are the called according to His purpose (Romans 8:28).

> For the children not yet being born, nor having done any good or evil, that the purpose of God according to election might stand, not of works but of Him who calls (Romans 9:11).

Calling is the allotment from God to tell you in which area He wants you to work in His kingdom. It is very important to stay within the boundaries of our calling. If we step into something for which we are not called, God is not responsible for providing for us nor to protect us. *Our provision is attached to our calling.*

Calling has to do with a specific group of people and a specific geographic location. When we study the lives of the people in the Bible, we see that they were called to function at a specific location. The reason we lack provision is because we are not functioning in our calling. We are operating based on our traditions or under the influence of the religious spirit. We do not see anyone in the Bible running around trying to do something to help fulfill what God has called them to do. If there is a calling, there is a provision.

> So when the Lord saw that he turned aside to look, God *called* to him from the midst of the bush and said, "Moses, Moses!" And he said, "Here I am" (Exodus 3:4).

God called Moses to fulfill His purpose through him. His purpose for him was to exercise dominion over Egypt; his calling was to deliver the people of Israel out of slavery. His gifts were many: miracles, governing, and signs and wonders. As previously mentioned, it is important to note that God calls us according to His purpose, not ours. His purpose never changes, which is to have dominion over the earth.

CALLING – THE KEY TO FULFILLING YOUR PURPOSE

CALLING

Many precious saints wait around and waste their lives, or they are waiting to be raptured out, thinking that they are not called by God. Many believe if God calls them, they will have a dramatic experience like an angel will appear to them or they will get hit by a bolt of lightning from the sky, or even have Jesus appear to them in person.

God gave such experience in the Bible because the people didn't have the written Word like we do today. The Word is God's purpose revealed to mankind. His Word is the ultimate authority, not any personal experience of an individual. If the Word says something about our lives, we better believe it!

> Therefore, brethren, be even more diligent to make your call and election sure, for if you do these things you will never stumble; for so an entrance will be supplied to you abundantly into the everlasting kingdom of our Lord and Savior Jesus Christ (2 Peter 1:10–11).

These verses say we need to give more diligence to make our *calling* and *election* sure. Nowhere in the Bible does it say we need to be diligent to make our *purpose* sure. Our purpose is already made clear by God. Nothing can be added to it; nothing can change it.

God called Samuel *(1 Samuel 3:4)*. Jesus called the disciples and Paul.

> And when He had *called* His twelve disciples to Him, He gave them power over unclean spirits, to cast them out, and to heal all kinds of sickness and all kinds of disease (Matthew 10:1).

Paul prayed that we would know the hope of our calling *(Ephesians 1:17–19)*. One thing about the people in the Bible is that they knew their purpose. They were not religiously brainwashed, as most of the

DISCOVERING PURPOSE, CALLING AND GIFTS

church is about their purpose. Every Jew knew why God put them on this planet. They were well versed in the first five books of the Bible and the prophets.

> Who has saved us and *called us* with a holy calling, not according to our works, but *according to His own purpose* and grace which was given to us in Christ Jesus before time began (2 Timothy 1:9).

If God saved us and called us before time began, that means the salvation and calling we received was planned by God before we were ever born! There is a general thinking that only some people are called and not others. That is a misconception. Every believer is called by God. Salvation and the call are something we receive at the same time. Another misunderstanding we have is that after we are saved, then a few years down the road we receive our calling. That is wrong as well.

If you are saved, you are called by God to do something specific in His kingdom. The primary purpose for God saving you was because He had something prepared for you to do. That is why the Bible says, "For we are His workmanship, created in Christ Jesus for good works, *which God prepared beforehand* that we should walk in them" *(Ephesians 2:10).*

I wasted many years of my life waiting for a burning bush experience or a Damascus road encounter, but nothing happened. There was no lightning from heaven, nor did an angel appear in my bedroom. I knew in my heart that I was called, but I was looking for assurance. I had to fight against doubt and unbelief.

If you are saved, you will know in your heart what you are called to do. Salvation and the call of God come in the same package, but not everybody is called to the same thing nor is everyone called into the ministry. God calls people to do all kinds of different things and not just ministry as we think of it. To God, everything we do is a ministry to Him.

When was Paul called into the ministry? When did he receive his salvation? His salvation and calling came at the same day and time. When were the disciples saved and called? Their salvation and calling came at the same moment when Jesus called them. Your salvation and call came at the same time as well.

God gave burning bush experiences in the Old Testament because the people were not saved as we are. They needed an external experience to confirm their calling because they did not have the indwelling of the Holy Spirit and Christ in them. Please do not misunderstand that. Even today, God might use an *experience* to call someone to do a specific task. The point is that we should not wait or look for this. Many look for such experiences because of doubt and unbelief. God is longsuffering and patient with us in all our shortcomings.

OUR CALLING IS VERY SPECIFIC

To fulfill your purpose, God calls you to do something specific. Everyone is called to do something different. Even if you are an apostle or a pastor, no apostle or pastor is called to do the same thing. In the 1980s, God used Dr. Cho in South Korea to establish the largest church in the world. He gave him the idea to start cell groups. People from all over the world came to South Korea to find out his secret.

They found out that the secret was the "cell system" they implemented. They took that idea and went back to their countries, and many churches tried to make it work as well. Why? Because they also wanted to have the largest church in the world. The sad thing is it did not work for them because it was a unique design God gave to Dr. Cho.

Apostle Paul and Peter were as different in their calling and ministries as night from day. They could not agree on many levels. It was not

DISCOVERING PURPOSE, CALLING AND GIFTS

that either of them was wrong; they were called to do different things and reach different groups of people.

God does not create copies; He creates only originals. When you try to copy someone, you lose your identity and calling. When God began to use Benny Hinn in a certain way, many servants of the Lord began to think, if I am really anointed, then I should do ministry like Benny does. They began to blow on people and shout "touch" when everybody was quiet in worship. They did not get the same result.

I heard some people even went so far as to stage ministry in their meetings, paying people to fall over when they blew or said touch. This got out of control, and many suffered shipwreck as a result. That is why Peter wrote that we should give all diligence to make sure your calling and election. He went through these experiences and challenges in his own life.

WHEN DOES GOD CALL US?

Though our calling was predetermined by God before the world began on earth, we come to the realization when we are saved. One thing I noticed in the Bible is that salvation and calling are inseparable. If you are saved, you are called. The sad thing today is that many get saved to go to heaven or to escape from hell, but no one gave an altar call to go to heaven or to escape from hell in the entire Bible.

The disciples and Paul were saved and called at the same time. God saves you because you have a calling on your life. He called you before the foundation of the world.

> Who has saved us and *called us* with a holy calling, not according to our works, but according to His own purpose and grace which was given to us in Christ Jesus before time began (2 Timothy 1:9).

CALLING – THE KEY TO FULFILLING YOUR PURPOSE

The Greek word for *calling* is *klesis*, which means a call or invitation.[19] That is the root of the word *ekklesia*, derived from *ek* in Greek, which means "out of." *Ekklesia* simply means "called out ones." God calls out certain people to fulfill His purpose.

God doesn't save you and then, ten years later, call you. They both come at the same time. God saved you to fulfill your calling. The problem is that many do not recognize their calling. What comes later is commissioning. What is commissioning?

COMMISSIONING

Calling and commissioning are two different things. Just because you are called does not mean you are commissioned to walk in your calling. Commissioning is usually done by other people who recognize your calling. Commissioning is *recognizing* or *releasing* you to walk in your calling. Most of the time, it is done by other apostles or prophets. God Himself may commission some people to do what He assigned them to do.

Paul was saved and called on the road to Damascus. He was commissioned, I believe, fourteen years later by the prophets and teachers from the church in Antioch *(Acts 13:1–2)*. However, he was preaching and teaching and planting churches long before he was commissioned.

That is why Jesus said many are called, but a few are chosen. Calling gives you the right to sign up for training. Then God takes us through a process of preparation through which many don't emerge. Any company that hires people to work for them takes them through

---

19 James Strong, "2821. Klésis," Biblehub.com, accessed January 19, 2019, https://biblehub.com/greek/2821.htm.

training. They want to make sure their employees are doing exactly what they want them to do.

The same system works in the kingdom. However, kingdom training is more severe and difficult, so be ready. To prepare you to pass all the spiritual tests you will ever go through, God has given me a powerful book that will help you graduate faster. It's called *Keys to Passing Your Spiritual Tests*.

TEN KEYS TO DISCOVERING YOUR CALLING

If God has a calling, how does He communicate that to us? Since no one can see God or has ever seen Him, how will we know and hear His voice? God has made ways to communicate His calling to us. He may not use the same way for everyone. He knows what to use for each person because each person is unique. There are ten major ways God uses to communicate His calling.

1. THE HOLY SPIRIT

Have you ever wished God would send someone to let us know exactly what He wants us to do? Maybe an angel, or a stranger, or our pastor, or anybody? That is what He did. He sent a person who knows everything to be our Helper and Counselor. There is a super-genius in all of heaven and on earth, and His name is Holy Spirit.

There is only one person on this earth that knows the purpose of your existence, and that is the Holy Spirit. He is the One who made you. The Bible says in 1 Corinthians 2:11 that no one knows what is in the mind of God except His Spirit. God sent His Holy Spirit to be with us and *in us*, to guide us into all truth.

But as it is written: "Eye has not seen, nor ear heard, nor have entered into the heart of man the things which God has prepared for those who love Him." But God has revealed them to us through His Spirit. For the Spirit searches all things, yes, the deep things of God. For what man knows the things of a man except the spirit of the man which is in him? Even so no one knows the things of God except the Spirit of God. Now we have received, not the spirit of the world, but the Spirit who is from God, that we might know the things that have been freely given to us by God (1 Corinthians 2:9–12).

The Holy Spirit knows everything about you. He is called Helper by Jesus *(John 14:26)*. Whenever you need help with anything, just ask, "Holy Spirit, please help me," and He will help you. The reason we do not get help is because we do not ask. He will not impose Himself to help you; He will stand beside you until you say something to Him.

2. DESIRE

The second key to discovering your calling is the desire in your heart. Most of the time, God communicates His calling by putting a desire in your heart. He does that between the ages of sixteen and twenty-five. You need to discover your calling between those ages and focus the rest of your life accomplishing that calling.

Desire is the seed to your destiny. God imprints an indelible desire in your heart, and it sticks with you for the rest of your life. You need to make sure it is the desire of your heart and spirit, not your head or a feeling that comes and goes after a few days. There is a difference between those and a fixed desire. The desire of your heart will not go away, but the desires of your head will change with every new circumstance or diminish over time. The Bible says to delight in the Lord, and He shall fulfill the desires of your heart *(Psalm 37:4)*.

3. GIFTING

What are you good at doing? Your gifting can be a clue to your calling. Many people are born with natural talents to do various things, and those could be a clue to your destiny. I did not grow up speaking English. I knew only three words in English until I was eighteen years old. Then I went to a Bible college in India. Within three months, God opened my understanding and gave me the English language as a gift. I began to speak and preach in English. God said, "You need this for your future." I did not know what my future was then.

Years went by, and I became more fluent in preaching in English than in my own native language. God gave me books to write, and when He gave me a message, He gave it in English. The reason is because the message God has given me is primarily for English-speaking people. I even dream in English. That was the clue to my purpose, but it took me a while to figure it out.

The gifting God gave you naturally by birth or spiritually when He called you is a clue to your calling. Sometimes God will use your natural gifting to fulfill your spiritual calling. What that means is that God might help you set up a business to provide for your call. God will equip you with the right gifts for your calling. You just need to trust Him and thank Him for it. Each person has at least one spiritual and natural gift. One will be to provide a source of income for you, and the other one is for you to serve others.

4. PASSION

You may not have a gifting or any special ability, but you have a passion to do or learn something. You need passion if you are serious about fulfilling your calling. When I was a teenager, I had the passion to learn European languages, like French and German. Every time I saw an ad in the newspaper for learning those languages, I told myself, "I need to go and join that school." But I never did it; I wish I had.

Also, make sure your passion is not a "strange passion." I have seen people with passion for all sorts of things. It may not be the right kind of passion. You may be passionate about crazy things. Passion needs to be based on knowledge and God's purpose for your life. It needs to be submitted to God just like everything else in our lives.

5. WHAT MAKES YOU ANGRY OR GRIEVED

You were born to solve a problem. What is the one thing that you would like to see changed? What makes you angry? What makes you grieved? What bothers you about life? Those are clues to your calling. After you decide what you want to do, you get the right education that helps you fulfill your calling.

I watched a movie about Mahatma Gandhi. He was from India, but was working as a lawyer in South Africa. One day while he was traveling by train, he happened to sit on a seat only permitted for whites. When the next station came, the people threw him out of the train. He was embarrassed and angry. That experience created a passion for his own people within him. During that time, his country was ruled by the British. He left South Africa, came to India, and began the historic fight for freedom. Eventually, his non-violent tactics worked, and he pushed the British out of India.

6. VOICE OF GOD

Sometimes God speaks to you directly through His Word or through someone else about your calling. We see that in the Bible, too. Sometimes God tells parents about the calling of their children. Their calling is so unique that they need an entirely different upbringing than normal children. During each critical juncture of your calling, you need to hear the voice of God and make the right choices in order to stay on track.

7. CIRCUMSTANCES

Your family background and where you were born can play a role in discovering and fulfilling your calling. Sometimes children take over their parent's business or ministry after their passing. It does not work like that all the time. I have seen children taking over ministries and businesses when they are not anointed to do so. God might have someone else in mind, but because of family ties, parents tend to put their children in position instead of the person God wants.

You may be a woman and think you do not have a passion to accomplish some big dream or achieve anything noteworthy, but your desire and dream is to be a wonderful wife and mother. That is perfectly fine. That is God's perfect will for your life, so be happy about it. Everyone is not created to do the extraordinary, but we are created to do what we do extraordinarily.

We should all be comfortable doing what God has directed without comparing ourselves to others. Some people become presidents or prime ministers, develop products, or make scientific breakthroughs. Others complete projects in their lives that the world may not notice as readily. Both are vital to God's plan. Each one is called to a completely different task.

8. YOUR RELATIONSHIPS

Another clue to your calling is who you are connected to and with which people you get along with best. People whom you connect with easily may not be the people from your own culture. You get along well with the people of your calling. God will give you supernatural favor with the people whom you are assigned to serve and bless. Paul was called to the Gentiles, but his passion was for the people from His culture. He kept going back to them, but each time he did, he got rejected and kicked out. When he went to the Gentiles, in most places, they welcomed him or had a supernatural breakthrough.

9. PROVISION

Where is your provision coming from? Who is God using to provide for you? Your provision is in the place of your calling. Your calling is in the place of your provision. God is committed to providing for you. He will always send someone to help you; it does not matter where you are. If there is no human available, He will send a bird, like the ravens God sent to Elijah.

10. DREAMS

Sometimes God will communicate your calling to you through your dreams. There are multiple examples of this in the Bible. We need to be open to God, however He chooses to communicate His calling. We cannot dictate to God as to what and how He must do it. He is God.

CHAPTER 15

GIFTS: THE KEY TO FULFILLING YOUR CALLING

> For the gifts and the calling of God are irrevocable
> *(Romans 11:29)*.

DISCOVERING AND DEVELOPING YOUR GIFTS

> But to each one of us grace was given according to the measure of Christ's gift (Ephesians 4:7).

> As each one has received a gift, minister it to one another, as good stewards of the manifold grace of God (1 Peter 4:10).

> For I wish that all men were even as I myself. But each one has his own gift from God, one in this manner and another in that (1 Corinthians 7:7).

Everyone has received gifts from God. Many have not recognized and developed them yet. Others, because of the intimidation of the enemy, are not using them to benefit themselves or others. They are hiding them like the person who received the one talent.

We could use many different names for them: gifts, talents, skills, abilities, and more. There are five different basic types of gifts. They are:

DISCOVERING PURPOSE, CALLING AND GIFTS

1. NATURAL GIFTS

I would call these the gifts of our body or the gifts given to us by our heavenly Father. People receive these gifts or special abilities at birth. Some have a natural ability to sing, draw, organize, see/know things prophetically, and much more. We need to recognize these gifts, and parents need to recognize them in their children by helping to develop them. That could be the secret to their prosperity.

When we had our children's home in India, there was a girl who was naturally gifted in drawing. She was not even ten years old, but she could draw like a professional. That was a natural gift God gave her at birth.

2. SPIRITUAL GIFTS

These are the gifts of the Holy Spirit, and they work through our spirit. He gives to whomever He wills. They are for the edification of the body of Christ and witness Jesus to the unreached. The religious spirit will make you feel insecure if you do not have a spiritual gift. For instance, if you cannot heal the sick and prophesy, it will make you feel like there is something wrong with you or that you are not spiritual enough, or that God does not love you enough. Those are the lies of the enemy.

> Now concerning spiritual *gifts,* brethren, I do not want you to be ignorant (1 Corinthians 12:1).

Spiritual gifts can be imparted. If someone has a spiritual gift, they can impart their gifts to others by laying their hands on them. This is especially true if that person is called to the fivefold ministry, like the Apostle Paul:

> For I long to see you, that I may impart to you some spiritual gift, so that you may be established (Romans 1:11).

God uses us to impart gifts to one another.

3. DEVELOPED SKILL AND TALENTS

People can develop skills and talents on their own, based on their interests. Some like the subject of mathematics, and they may want to pursue it to become better in it. Eventually, they can do things such as become a math teacher, go into accounting and start a business, start online tutoring to students who are struggling in math, or get a job as a statistician or in marketing. The possibilities are endless.

I was reading the news about the Winter Olympics and its contestants. It said someone had been preparing eight long years for a hundred-second competition. That means they had been working and focused on this for eight years; the first hundred seconds of their competition would determine whether they received a medal or not. We have the ability to have that kind of determination if we choose.

4. MOTIVATIONAL GIFTS

This refers to the gifts of our soul or the gifts given to us by Jesus. These gifts come with our born-again experience. Gifts of the Holy Spirit come with the baptism of the Holy Spirit. There are seven motivational gifts mentioned in Romans 12:

> Having then gifts differing according to the grace that is given to us, let us use them: if prophecy, let us prophesy in proportion to our faith; or ministry, let us use it in our ministering; he who teaches, in teaching; he who exhorts, in exhortation; he who gives, with liberality; he who leads, with diligence; he who shows mercy, with cheerfulness (Romans 12:6–8).

5. MINISTRY GIFTS

These are special gifts Jesus gives to His body to grow and mature believers to become everything God created them to be. They also bring up the body of Christ to manifest the fullness of Christ to the world. There are five ministry gifts mentioned in Ephesians 4:11. Some say there are only four. Their responsibilities are mentioned below.

Your money is in developing and using your gifts. Do you want to know why many remain poor? Because they do not use their gifts. If you look at people with lots of money, you will find that for many, their gifts brought them that money, although some accumulated by lying and cheating.

When you have developed or mastered a gift, people will pay you to receive that service or benefit from you. It's like fruit on a tree. That fruit is for others to enjoy. Gifts are your fruit. The good news is that God has given at least one gift to every human being. He will not create anyone without putting at least one gift in them or giving them an opportunity to develop one.

It doesn't matter where you were born and into what financial background; nothing can stop you from using your gift. Your gift will work in any circumstance or culture. It will require three to five years of dedicated commitment to master a gift, skill, or talent. Once you master a gift, you will become a treasure house. People will search you out to find you because they need your service to solve a problem they have. They will travel the seas to find you.

Remember the parable of the talents? It is the last parable mentioned in Luke 19. Jesus was going to leave the earth after finishing His assignment, and He wanted to make sure He was not leaving them empty-handed. As God, He was telling them He was leaving them

GIFTS: THE KEY TO FULFILLING YOUR CALLING

with gifts, which He wanted them to use in business and multiply. That is God's heart for you. Whatever gift or talent you have received, you should use.

What is business? Business is a system of operation through which you receive an intended product or result. After you discover your gift, you need to put a plan in place to use that gift systematically so that you can profit from it and multiply it. If you do not, you will remain poor. Jesus is not against doing business with the gift He gave you; in fact, He commanded us to do that. If we do not, He will not be happy. He will take the gift He gave and give it to someone else who is using it and multiplying it.

God has not put any limit on how many gifts we can have. It's up to us. The more we are faithful with what we have, the more He will give us. The more you use what you have, the more new gifts will be added to you. As long as you do not use what you have, do not expect any increase on any level.

There was a season in my life when I thought I had not received any gifts at all, especially when I was a teenager. I did not know which gift I had as my natural gift. I was comparing my life with others who were using their natural gifts. I was not good at any of the things they did well, so I felt useless and became very discouraged.

I did not have the maturity to understand that I was strong in areas others were not. I was not good at sports or music, though I tried and wanted to be good at both. What I did not realize was that I was born to lead. My gift was organizing and administration, necessities for leadership roles.

When I was born again, I received motivational gifts. Then when I was baptized in the Holy Spirit, I received gifts of the Holy Spirit, and when I stepped into the ministry, I received the ministry gifts. Now,

DISCOVERING PURPOSE, CALLING AND GIFTS

I believe I have at least these gifts. The more I use them, the better I become, and God gives me more.

The best thing to do is to start where you are and start using what you have received. I started as a Sunday school teacher for little kids, and then in cleaning the church building and doing the organizing for youth meetings and Sunday morning services. That's when God began to add more gifts to my life. As long as you wait, you will be the loser. *The moment you break free from fear and intimidation, the new future that you have been waiting for all your life begins.* Today is the day of salvation and breakthrough. Do not waste or wait for another day.

Start where you are and with what you have. You always have what you need to start what God has called you to do. Don't get trapped into the illusion that you are missing something, or lacking something, or need someone, or any other traps the enemy has been using to make you feel handicapped. Don't wait until you can do something perfectly, either. They are all lies and tricks to steal your effectiveness and your destiny.

Just because you have a gift that does not mean everything will become easy, and you do not need to put any effort into it. The opposite is true. Life is a constant fight. Become tough on your mind. The Bible calls it girding the loins of our minds *(1 Peter 1:13)*. If we can overcome the battle in our mind, victory is guaranteed. Many wait for the outside circumstances to change first. *Change and victory needs to take place in our mind first—before it happens anywhere else.*

Focus on whatever gifts, talents, or skills you want to grow in. Focus five years on one gift or talent and master it. If you start when you are fifteen, by the time you reach thirty, you will have at least three gifts or skills in which you excel. You will not have to beg anybody for anything. People and resources will follow you.

YOUR GIFT WILL MAKE ROOM FOR YOU

A man's gift makes room for him, and brings him before great men (Proverbs 18:16).

This verse says a man's gift, not his purpose or calling, will make room for him and bring him before great men. It is possible to discover your purpose and calling and still find that nobody knows who you are, but you cannot discover your gifts and remain hidden. Exercising your gifting will attract people to you. Finding and exercising your gift is the key to having influence. That's when you will begin to prosper. It is important that you spend time developing and sharpening your gift(s). The enemy will try his best to intimidate you to prevent you from using them. Break off his hold and come out of the cave.

Feeding the sheep was David's job. The only benefit he received from his job was that his expenses were covered. But he was a smart boy. He used the spare time he had while doing his job to develop skills and identify his gifts. He was unaware that he was preparing for an opportunity to be presented to him to exercise those gifts. It was his gifts that opened the door for him to be brought to the palace to stand before the king.

What brought him to the palace was not his job as a shepherd but his skills and gifting. David's gifts brought him before kings. That is why the Bible says, "Do you see a man skillful and experienced in his work? He will stand before kings; he will not stand before obscure men" *(Proverbs 22:29).*

Since we all have one purpose, we need to know our calling and gifting.

Therefore, brethren, be even more diligent to make your call and election sure, for if you do these things you will never stumble (2 Peter 1:10).

THE ULTIMATE CALLING

Here is the ultimate purpose for all of us. You might be a doctor, housewife, mailman, businessman, minister, or anything else, but your ultimate calling is to reveal Jesus Christ to this world. The whole creation is waiting for the manifestation of the sons of God. We have been called to be transformed into the image and likeness of the Son of God.

When you read the Bible and study the people God used, they are all pictures and types of Jesus Christ. That list includes kings, queens, shepherds, statesmen, prophets, deliverers, leaders, warriors: all men and women of faith. Everything that was made and written in the Bible was to reveal Christ the Son of God. All creation reveals the glory of God.

While on this earth, Jesus said, "I am in the Father and the Father in Me" *(John 14:11)*. He also said, "He who has seen Me has seen the Father" *(John 14:9)*. Read the following verses carefully.

> No one has seen God at any time. The only begotten Son, who is in the bosom of the Father, He has declared *Him* (John 1:18).

> And that day [the day Holy Spirit comes] you will know that I am in My Father, and *you in Me, and I in you* (John 14:20).

> If anyone loves Me, he will keep My word; and My Father will love him, and *We will come to him and make Our home with him* (John 14:23).

If it is true that those who have seen Jesus have seen the Father *because* the Father is in Jesus and Jesus is in the Father, then it follows that those who have seen us have seen Jesus *because* in the same way, we are in Jesus and He is in us.

If the world is to believe the Father has sent Jesus to the earth, the following needs to happen. It already happened, but the church needs to receive and walk in that revelation.

> That they all may be one, as *You*, Father, are in Me, and I in *You;* that they also may be one in Us, that the world may believe that *You sent* Me (John 17:21).

> So Jesus said to them again, "Peace to you! As the Father has *sent* Me, I also send you" (John 20:21).

Jesus told His disciples that as the Father had sent Him, He was sending them! For what purpose? To reveal Jesus! *If Jesus was sent to reveal the Father, we are sent to reveal Jesus.*

Apostle Paul wrote, "If anyone is in Christ, *he is* a new creation; old things have passed away; behold, all things have become new" *(2 Corinthians 5:17)*. In another place, he wrote, "Christ is in us the hope of glory" *(Colossians 1:27)*. If we are in Christ and Christ is in us, those who see us should see Jesus. We need to think like this, or only our actions will change. Most are more conscious of their old man (the old self before we were saved) than their born-again spirit man and the new nature we have received. Put off the old man with all its traits, and put on the new man created in Christ Jesus.

Say this out loud: "I put off the old man I received through natural birth, and I put on the new man created in Christ Jesus."

The Bible says that "he who is joined to the Lord [born again] is one spirit *with Him" (1 Corinthians 6:17)*. My spirit is one with Jesus Christ.

DISCOVERING PURPOSE, CALLING AND GIFTS

We have the mind of Christ. "For who has known the mind of the Lord that he may instruct Him? But we have the mind of Christ" *(1 Corinthians 2:16).*

We are one flesh and one body with Jesus. "For we are members of His body, of His flesh and of His bones. For this reason a man shall leave his father and mother and be joined to his wife, and the two shall become one flesh. *This is a great mystery, but I speak concerning Christ and the church" (Ephesians 5:30–32).*

According to the Bible, we are one spirit, one mind (soul) and one flesh (body) with Jesus. Do you see how we are cheated by the devil and the religious spirit in the church? We have to shake off our pathetic visage and poverty spirit and believe and act what the Word says about us instead. We are not just saved to make it to heaven. We have been saved to the uttermost, which means *everything* is saved. The Father is in us, and Jesus is in us; we are in Jesus, and the Holy Spirit is in us and upon us. What else does God have to do for us? May God open our eyes to see the truth!

The Bible says our body is the temple of the Holy Spirit and it is sealed by Him for the day of redemption *(1 Corinthians 3:16; Ephesians 1:13–14).*

You might have heard this saying: "The only Jesus people will see is us." That is a true statement and the essence of all Christianity and all the Christian things we do! No matter what your calling and giftings are, the ultimate purpose we have is to reveal Jesus to those around us. If they do not see Jesus, we failed in our mission.

If you are called to be a businessman, sportsman, entertainer, hairdresser, pastor, housewife, mother, or construction worker, you need to reveal Jesus through that. There is an aspect of Jesus that can be revealed through every profession. When I say reveal Jesus, I do not mean saying, "Hallelujah! Praise the Lord!" to everyone you see or all your customers. Francis of Assisi once said, "Preach the gospel at all times and if necessary, use words."

It is not preaching fire and brimstone to everyone you see and all your friends. It is being the light and salt of the earth. The reason God created you was to manifest His glory. All creation manifests His glory. But each of them is different in their glory as Paul taught in 1 Corinthians 15:40–41.

Jesus spoke to His Father at the end of His ministry, saying, "I have glorified You on the earth. I have finished the work which You have given me to do" *(John 17:4)*. That is the way we manifest His glory; we do everything with excellence and finish the work God gave us to do.

Once you discover your calling, the next thing to do in order to fulfill it is to recognize God's timing. This is vital and will save you from a lot of headaches and unnecessary loss. I do not have enough room to explain all that in this book. Please get a copy of my book, **Recognizing God's Timing for Your Life**, to learn more.

CHAPTER 16

SEVEN REASONS FOR POVERTY

1. MISUNDERSTANDING OF PURPOSE, CALLING, AND GIFTS

I believe by now you understand the importance of purpose, calling, and gifts. The majority of people do not function based on them. They are in survival mode. They have been conditioned by their culture to go to school and then look for a job to make some money. All they care about is making some money to make a living. When you do not understand your purpose, the only way to live is to survive and die.

2. LACK OF VISION

As the Bible says, where there is no vision, people perish *(Proverbs 29:18)*. The reason many do not accept the vision God gives them is because they compare the vision with their current reality and conclude it's never going to happen or be possible. Vision is a picture or blueprint of your unseen future that has not materialized yet. All you have to do is believe it; that's the most difficult part. Once you believe it, things will automatically begin to happen that propel you toward fulfilling it.

Every architect creates a blueprint before beginning a construction project. Once the blueprint is ready, in the mind of the architect, the building is completed. Then when he begins the construction, he starts it from the finishing point.

One quality Abraham, the father of our faith, had, was that whenever God showed him a picture of his future, he believed it like a child. There was nothing in the natural for him to support it, but He believed the Author of it because he knew God was faithful.

3. LACK OF KNOWLEDGE

Everybody knows something about a lot of things, but many do not know enough about anything to monetize their knowledge. When the Bible says God's people perished for lack of knowledge, it has more than one meaning. First, it means they do not know who they are in God and what He has given to them, so the enemy deceives them and keeps them ignorant. Second, it means they lack specialized knowledge in any specific area of life, so they can't get paid for what they know.

4. LACK OF DILIGENCE

What is diligence? Why does the Bible use the word diligence instead of hard work? Diligence is a combination of hard work with excellence, focus, and innovation. Just by hard work, people won't overcome poverty. I have seen many hardworking people that remain poor. They keep doing the same thing over and over again, thinking some day they are going to make more money, not understanding the value of the land or the resources it contains and how to maximize them.

5. LAZINESS

Laziness is a spiritual issue as well as a disease. I think people who are lazy don't want to be lazy; they can't help themselves. They need deliverance. I believe laziness is a spirit, just like poverty.

SEVEN REASONS FOR POVERTY

> The hand of the diligent will rule, but the lazy man will be put to forced labor (Proverbs 12:24).

> Laziness casts one into a deep sleep, and an idle person will suffer hunger (Proverbs 19:15).

The difference between a lazy and slothful person is that the slothful person does what he does halfheartedly while the lazy person refuses to do anything. He always blames someone or something.

6. NEGLECT OR MISUSE OF OPPORTUNITIES

Many people think they are poor because they are underprivileged or did not have all the opportunities that rich people had. Keep in mind: Rich people did not have all those opportunities when they were not rich. Many people think they are not as talented or educated as others. As we have already learned, God gave each person a gift. There is no one who can make an excuse before God on the day of judgment.

> I returned and saw under the sun that—the race is not to the swift, nor the battle to the strong, nor bread to the wise, nor riches to men of understanding, nor favor to men of skill; but time and chance happen to them all (Ecclesiastes 9:11).

7. NOT MAXIMIZING RESOURCES FROM GOD

Next to people, land is the most expensive resource God gave us. Everything we use, eat, drink, and breathe comes out of the land. In many countries, people don't take care of their land. They are waiting for someone to come and give them something for free. They do not understand the value of land or how to make it productive. They might be walking and sitting on a treasure of an oil well or a diamond mine,

DISCOVERING PURPOSE, CALLING AND GIFTS

but they have no discernment to recognize it. For generations, they have been struck with poverty.

Our hands can create miracles. There is no limit to the number of things our hands and fingers can do. The only problem is that they are not trained yet. Let's make a difference for God and His kingdom on the earth by fulfilling our purpose by discovering and flowing in what we are called to do by maximizing the gifts, talents, and resources He gave us. Let's take back what the enemy stole from us and the generations before us. Let's honor God by accomplishing His will on earth as it is in heaven.

Once we are released to fulfill our purpose and calling, our assignment is connected to discipling a town, city, or nation. That is what we will be learning in the next chapter.

CHAPTER 17
DISCIPLING NATIONS–TRUE DISCIPLESHIP

> Go therefore and make disciples of all the nations, baptizing them in the name of the Father and of the Son and of the Holy Spirit *(Matthew 28:19)*.

For a long time I understood this as if Jesus said, "Go therefore and make disciples *from* all nations." I always focused on an individual mandate. Jesus did not give an individual mandate. He gave a *national* mandate: *discipling nations*. He did not say *from* all nations but *of* all nations. We are supposed to disciple nations. How do we do that? Is that even possible in our day and age?

To answer that question, we need to understand what discipleship is and how to do it. I could write a whole book on that subject alone!

WHAT IS TRUE DISCIPLESHIP?

How did the early church disciple nations like Syria, Turkey, and many present-day western countries that were once Christian? When the church lost its purpose and became a mere building-focused religious entity instead of *functioning* as a kingdom embassy, we lost nations and cities.

DISCOVERING PURPOSE, CALLING AND GIFTS

Though there are thousands of religious entities (more churches exist today than at any other time in the history of Christianity) functioning on almost every corner, they have no influence on what is happening either in the spiritual or natural realm. We have left our *first love* (Jesus), our *first mandate* (to rule and reign on earth), and the *Great Commission* (to disciple nations).

When we talk about discipling nations and cities, it may seem like an impossible dream to many, but let me tell you that nothing is impossible with our God. The problem is that we lack the capacity to believe Him to do something. God is looking for a group of people to believe for something that only He can do, but we are so programmed in our religious and rapture mindset that when we hear anything contrary, we have a tendency to oppose it.

How did the early church disciple cities like Ephesus, Corinth, and Rome? I will answer that in the next pages. Idol worshippers, temples, and government institutions were brought under the feet of Jesus. We are not talking about something new here. What I am sharing has happened before in history, and if it happened once, there is the possibility of it happening again.

If we do not disciple our nations, someone else will do it. The devil will use his children to disciple our cities and nations, and our children. There is no point in blaming anyone for how things are going in our nations because we let it happen.

Everywhere I go, I meet people who are unhappy with the direction their cities and nations are headed. They are not happy about what is happening in their schools and neighborhoods. They are helpless, and all they do is complain and murmur. This book is intended to train you to act, not just gain information and then run and find another book without doing anything about what you just learned. If you keep doing that, you will become spiritually barren and a religious junkie.

DISCIPLING NATIONS–TRUE DISCIPLESHIP

The church with a revival mindset thinks if they go to a park with a guitar and sing five songs, God will come down and do something for their city. That is a religious deception. That is not the way the first-century church operated. They operated with a kingdom mindset.

I use an example of an airplane to show people what is happening in our nations and why our culture is going from bad to worse. It is easy to blame the devil, but he is doing what he is supposed to do. The problem is that we are not doing what we are created to do. I hope and pray this book will inspire you to *do* something.

Imagine traveling in an intercontinental airplane and the passengers in the cabin are the church. Suppose there are five hundred passengers, and they are all seated comfortably. They all have the same destination; spiritually speaking, it is heaven. No one can jump off of that plane in the middle of the trip. Once you get in and it takes off, you are stuck until it lands.

These believers are singing and having revivals. They shout, "Praise the Lord" and "Hallelujah" every time they meet a new believer. They sing songs with lyrics like, "We are going to meet the King!" Good food and entertainment are available every now and then. They are meeting new people, creating friendships, and everything is going smoothly.

What they do not realize is that their lives depend on the two people in the cockpit. Those two people decide almost everything for them—what they eat, when they eat, how much air they can breathe, when they sit down, when they can stand up, how often they can move around in the cabin, what kind of entertainment they can watch, when they can watch it, and what news they can hear. Everything is controlled from that cockpit. Their fate depends on those two people.

The sad thing is that the passengers pay those two guys and their company to make all of the decisions for them. That is what is happening

DISCOVERING PURPOSE, CALLING AND GIFTS

in our lives and nations. Though we have had many revivals, rallies, and crusades, nothing changes for the better because all the major decisions are made by the people who are in the *cockpits* of our nations, cities, and government buildings. The reason the situation is going from bad to worse is because most of these people who make decisions for us are the embodiment of Satan himself.

We elected these people to their offices. We pay them to make those decisions for us; unless we replace them with those who will make good and right decisions, nothing will change for the better. That is what we need to do right now. We should have done it years ago, but we let it go this long.

Who is discipling our nations and children? Corrupt politicians, media moguls, business tycoons, celebrities, and others who are in the cockpits of our nations. Every aspect of our society has a cockpit, those people that make decisions for the rest of society. Just because we gather in a building on Sunday morning for an hour and a half and shout doesn't necessarily cause things to change for the better.

There are various ways to disciple a nation. How many people do you think someone like Michael Jackson discipled through his musical skills? Millions of people all over the world. How many people has Steve Jobs discipled through his products? How many children have been discipled by J.K. Rowling? Or McDonald's? How many people and nations are discipled by communism or socialism?

For too long, we have limited our methods of discipling to preaching and teaching; these days, people are not very interested in that. Not everyone will listen to our preaching, but everybody needs and is interested in something. Seeing and meeting those needs is very critical in the process of discipling a nation.

Keep in mind that any time we leave a gap empty in our society, the enemy will bring something from his storehouse to fill it. We have neglected our gates and left the doors open for the enemy to bring anything he wants through them to influence our culture.

There is a lot of talk and training on discipleship. When I was a young Christian, I was told that reading the Bible, witnessing, praying, being a good Christian, and going to church on Sunday morning was discipleship. If I practiced those habits, I was considered a good Christian or a disciple of Jesus Christ.

Based on the above qualifications, any religious person would be considered a good disciple of Jesus, but that is not true. I don't know how people came up with that idea. When we study the lives of those discipled, or mentored, by others in the Bible, we see a totally different picture.

How did Jesus disciple His twelve disciples? Did He give them a Bible (Torah) reading plan? Did He ask them to pray for a certain amount of time each day? Were they instructed to go to the temple on every Sabbath? No.

According to the Bible, we see that discipleship was practiced for an entirely different reason. It was not for any religious reason. It was not intended for taking people to heaven. From the discipleship program of Jesus Christ, we understand the following purposes.

Why did Jesus select twelve disciples? Was the intent to turn them into "good Christians"? What benefit would He get if there were a bunch of good Christians walking around the streets of Jerusalem? In fact, there are millions of them in our day and time.

We are going to look at discipleship from a kingdom perspective. The reason Jesus selected the Twelve was because the number twelve is the number of government in the Bible. He could have selected any number of people, but He specifically chose only twelve. He needed a governing body, and whatever God does has a kingdom flavor because He is a King. From the biblical pattern of discipleship, we see the following principles evident.

RELEASING PEOPLE INTO THEIR DESTINY

The first thing Jesus did for the disciple was to release them into their destiny. That is the initiation process of discipleship. If there is no destiny, there is no discipleship. Discipleship must be geared toward releasing people into their destiny; otherwise, it is not true discipleship.

The devil stole our destinies through Adam. Ever since Adam lost the battle, the majority of people on earth go down into eternity without fulfilling their purpose. Cemeteries are filled with potentials and dreams that were never realized. Through the coming of the last Adam, we got the opportunity to be restored and walk out our destiny.

Peter, Andrew, James, and John were fishermen, and they were stuck with a job over which they did not have any control. They were at the mercy of nature and their learned skill, or even luck, if they were to catch any fish. If they did not make a catch, they went hungry.

That's the situation with many of us, too. We are at the mercy of other people and circumstances. That's not the way to live our lives. We should function only at the mercy of God. We have to be accountable and responsible to others.

Jesus set these men free from the tyranny of luck and fate and released them into their destiny. They became the founding apostles of the *ekklesia* of Jesus Christ on earth. They received the revelation of the kingdom of God in the form of a seed. We are supposed to be enjoying the fruit of it, but we have a lot of catching up to do. Unfortunately, we have to build on the foundation again because of the destruction caused by the religious spirit.

DISCIPLING NATIONS–TRUE DISCIPLESHIP

Millions of people in our society are stuck in jobs and circumstances they do not enjoy. They feel trapped with no way out. Their hearts are crying out for freedom, and they are looking for a Deliverer, just like the Israelites looked for a deliverer when they were in bondage in Egypt. Many are under the yokes of addiction, abuse, and debt. They know they need freedom, but they do not know how or from where to get it. Setting those people free from their bondages and releasing them into the destiny God has for them is the first step to discipleship.

Their destinies have been taken captive, some to the survival system (jobs), religious system, habits, sin, their past, or any other tool the enemy can use. That is why Jesus said He came to set the captives free. Once they are released into their destiny, we need to train them to navigate life and fulfill their destiny. That is the process of discipleship.

Discipleship is not always about preparing people to be in ministry, but releasing them to do whatever God created them to do. Often we have limited it to religious purposes, and we need to remove those limitations before we go any further. Everything we do and every way we as believers function is rooted and founded on those twelve men that Jesus chose and discipled and their teachings.

There is no particular length of time needed to disciple another person. Sometimes it takes just one meeting and an impartation to change someone's life for the better. Many times, throughout my life, I have had the experience of meeting someone, and grace was imparted to him or her, and their life was changed for the better. Each case is unique and will vary.

Below are some examples of people who were discipled by others and released into their destiny. God, in turn, used them to disciple nations.

After Paul's conversion, Jesus appeared to a man called Ananias and told him to go and meet Paul. Actually, it was to disciple him.

DISCOVERING PURPOSE, CALLING AND GIFTS

He was hesitant at first because of the news he had heard about Paul persecuting the church.

Nevertheless, in obedience to the vision, Ananias went to Paul and released him into his destiny. He laid hands on him, and Paul received the Holy Spirit. The rest is history. Paul went around establishing churches that discipled cities and nations. That is the power of true discipleship. It doesn't take a lifetime to release someone into his or her destiny.

Joshua was discipled by Moses, and it was done with one intention. Once Moses was done with his job, Joshua was to pick up where he left off and continue in his footsteps. Joshua was released into his destiny. He discipled the people of Israel to possess the Promised Land.

Elijah discipled Elisha, and he was released into his destiny. He, in turn, discipled the nation of Israel and other kings. If you look at any example in the Bible, the disciple was released into his or her destiny.

Esther was discipled by her cousin, Mordecai, and when the time and opportunity came, he released her into her destiny. She was instrumental in discipling the kingdom of Persia and the Jewish nation.

If you study other examples in the Bible, you will see the same pattern. John the Baptist discipled Jesus by releasing Him into His destiny at the baptism in the Jordan.

In today's system of discipleship, people have been abused and misused by the personal agenda of the one discipling them. They have them polish their shoes and carry their bags and give massages to their master or their mistress, and they never get released into their destiny. That is not biblical discipleship; it is slavery or servanthood.

Every time people had an encounter with God, they were released into their destiny as well. Abraham, Moses, Gideon, Paul, and many others were propelled into their calling. That is what should happen to us at salvation. At the moment of salvation, people should have an encounter with their Savior that should release them into their destiny.

We have inherited a wrong understanding of salvation as well. We have limited salvation to a ticket to reach heaven, like buying fire insurance. Then the rest of our lives we live in fear of losing that insurance by doing something wrong. Nobody can live effectively for God with that kind of belief system. Salvation is not a reward for good merits or for religious works. It's a gift. We know what we need to do to receive a gift from someone: just have a heart to receive and be thankful for it.

RELEASING PEOPLE TO DISCIPLE CITIES AND NATIONS

Why do we need to release people into their destinies? Nations are made of people. Each nation and city also has a divine destiny. Most nations are not fulfilling their destinies because the people in those nations are not fulfilling their personal destinies. When the people of a nation are released into their destinies, they in turn will disciple their nation by releasing its destiny.

Anything and everything we do, whether it's evangelism, missions, government, business, charity work, or anything at all, must be geared toward discipling our cities and nations. Western civilization became so busy building megachurches and cathedrals that they neglected to disciple their cities and nations. As a result, we lost them.

Western countries sent missionaries throughout the world with a passion to save souls and take them to heaven. Unfortunately, they neglected their own nations and didn't even teach the souls they'd won about their responsibility and how to disciple their cities and nations.

DISCOVERING PURPOSE, CALLING AND GIFTS

Why do nations go through financial ruin and other chaos? It is because the citizens become selfish and self-centered and have no vision for their nation. They steal the resources from their nation and sell them to multinational companies. They rob their own people and abuse them.

As disciples are released into their destinies, they must focus on releasing the destinies of their cities and nations. Most Christians have no vision for their own country. They only have a vision for heaven and are longing to walk on streets of gold and live in their heavenly mansions. They are looking for something for free.

Every discipleship program needs to be geared toward one purpose, which is eventually to disciple nations. For too long, our discipleship programs have been focused on producing *good* Christians who were mostly useless to their countries. There was no such discipleship in the Bible. Many believers are waiting to go to heaven and are more concerned about what is happening in heaven than on earth.

Now the question is: How do we disciple nations?

When we release people into their destiny, we are helping to fulfill the destiny of that nation. How do we release people into their destiny?

- By helping them discover their purpose
- By helping them realize their calling
- By helping them identify their gifts or imparting gifts

In the same way every individual has a divine destiny, each town, city, and nation also has its own destiny. Believers need to receive a blueprint from heaven for their towns and cities, then manifest or build according to the blueprint God has for them, making each aspect of those cities as it is in heaven.

DISCIPLING NATIONS—TRUE DISCIPLESHIP

How do we disciple a town, a city, or a nation? Before I answer that question, my question to you is, "Who is discipling our cities and nations right now?"

We can use a variety of methods and tools to disciple a city or a nation. For example, the town I live in is discipled by a private Christian school. It is one of the best schools I have seen in the world, and their motto is "Influence through Excellence."

We could use businesses, products, media, skills, or even government to disciple a nation or town. When I was in Bulgaria, the local leader took the ministry team to visit a nearby slum. It was a heartbreaking experience. We saw hundreds of families with children trying to survive. I saw more children per family than I have ever seen anywhere else.

Every slum has the same culture: dirt, disorder, chaos, hopelessness, and loud music. We had a medical doctor from France with us who had been involved in community development in many parts of Africa. After our visit, there was a time to debrief on our experience and come up with any possible solutions to solve the problems for that slum. Different people expressed different ideas on what could be done to help the people.

When the time came for this doctor to share her ideas, she came up with six needs this slum (or any other slum) has. The first thing she spoke of was the need for basic hygiene. I was surprised she didn't say they needed the gospel, or Jesus, or another church in that community. She spoke of their actual needs first because she has a kingdom mindset.

That struck me, and I began to think about why she said hygiene. I don't think that if we had gone there with the religious gospel that very many people would have showed any interest or received it, but if

DISCOVERING PURPOSE, CALLING AND GIFTS

we had done something to help them with any of their existing needs, that would open the door to share the gospel.

When Jesus called the disciples, He didn't ask if they wanted to go to heaven when they died. Instead, He met their immediate need. Their need was to catch some fish to survive another day. He gave them what they needed, and it opened their hearts to receive Him. Then He released them to fulfill their kingdom destiny. As a result, they left everything and followed Him.

We read and studied the price and size of discipleship but not on the purpose of it. I remember reading different books on the price of discipleship when I was starting in the ministry. They were all good books, but none of them mentioned releasing people into their destinies. They were all focused on the religious experience, habits, and becoming a "gooder" Christian. Say three "Praise the Lords!" a day; after discipleship, they were trained to say it five times a day and a little louder.

I heard about an interesting incident that took place in India. Christians in this particular community faced horrible persecution from Hindu fanatics. Their houses and church buildings were burned to the ground. Many of them were beaten and killed. When this persecution began to subside, the ministers and ministries began to think about how to continue ministry in that particular place again. People were not open to hearing the normal preaching. Additionally, they had warnings from the militia that no religious conversion or evangelistic meetings were permitted.

God gave an idea to one of the ministers. Most of the people in that community were illiterate. The idea was to share the gospel through storytelling. They chose different stories and parables of Jesus and began to share them with the people on their level. They didn't need to attend a particular church meeting.

They shared these stories as part of normal everyday life. When people went to work, they shared these stories with those who were working with them. Ladies began to share stories with their neighbors. Farmers and quarry workers shared stories with their coworkers. The momentum began to build, and people wanted to know more stories and the source of those stories. They shared Jesus with them, and many came to the Lord because of that. The only problem was that all these discipleship programs were geared toward taking people to heaven or converting them from one religion to another.

RELEASING THE DESTINY OF THEIR NATIONS

Why do people in a nation need to be released into their destinies? As a corporate body, they can release the destiny of their nations. Each nation is unique and has a divine destiny just like each individual has a unique destiny.

We talk about the American dream, Chinese food, Indian spices, French fries, German cars, Japanese technology, Canadian bacon, and Colombian coffee. Each nation is known for something. However, they are not necessarily God's destinies for those nations. As believers, we have to recognize what each nation is known for in heaven and accomplish that will on earth.

Why did nations in the Western Hemisphere become godless societies? They were so focused on building big church buildings, cathedrals, and worldwide organizations that they forgot to disciple their nations. While they proceeded to "evangelize" the rest of the world, they left their own countries open to the enemies. They came in and took over the cockpits of their cities and nations.

When you disciple a nation, that nation will fulfill its God-given destiny, just as an individual who is a disciple will fulfill their destiny.

DISCOVERING PURPOSE, CALLING AND GIFTS

How do we disciple a nation? We need to receive a blueprint from heaven concerning the destiny of that nation. Everything we do has to be according to the blueprint in heaven.

As it is in heaven, so be it on earth. As Jesus said, "I do what I see My Father doing." That should be our motto as well. That is true ministry. Many are caught up in doing so many things, thinking they are in ministry or ministering and helping God, but that's not ministry. Anyone who was called into ministry was called to do something specific. God gave them a specific assignment.

WHY NATIONS?

God is interested in nations, not just people. He is the One who started all nations. He wants nations to serve Him. Nations are Jesus' inheritance.

> I will declare the decree: The Lord has said to Me, "You are My Son, today I have begotten You. Ask of Me, and I will give You the nations for *Your inheritance*, and the ends of the earth for Your possession" (Psalm 2:7–8).

This is a promise to Jesus from His Father. We are part of fulfilling that promise for Jesus. Many have taken those verses personally and claimed nations for their own inheritance and for their ministries. That is not what those verses mean. When we ask for nations, we are asking for them *for Jesus*. For example, if we are asking for the United States of America, we should say something like this. "Father, I ask for the United States of America as an inheritance for Jesus Christ my King." All things are through Him and for Him and by Him.

Hebrews 11 is about the people of faith and what they did. In verse 33, it says, "Who through faith subdued kingdoms, worked righteousness, obtained promises, stopped the mouth of lions." The first thing these disciples did was subdue kingdoms or nations. *Your calling and gifts are connected to discipling a particular nation.*

I was surprised that it said the first thing they did as a result of exercising their faith was to subdue kingdoms or nations. Why did it not say how many souls they won for God or how many worship concerts they conducted? God's priority is nations and their destinies, both now and in the past. His heart is longing for the restoration of nations back to Him. He wants to be their King and rule over them. He is the King of all nations. That is why Jesus told us to go and disciple nations, not make converts that are waiting go to heaven.

RESTORING THE EARTH TO ITS ORIGINAL STATE

We have inherited a doom, gloom, and despair eschatology for the nations. I do not believe that is what Jesus taught. The Bible speaks of restoration, not destruction. Our God is a God of restoration and redemption. What joy will He receive if He destroyed all nations? That would be the utmost loss. I believe God will extend every chance He can to restore someone or a nation back to Him.

The Bible says God will hold back Jesus until the time for the restoration of all things, which every holy prophet has spoken of since the world began.

> Whom heaven must receive until the times of restoration of all things, which God has spoken by the mouth of all His holy prophets since the world began (Acts 3:21).

This is very clear about what God is thinking about creation. He is planning to restore all things, not destroy all things. Discipling nations is a part of that process.

DISCIPLING THE NATIONS BY SENDING THEM INTO THE WORLD

In Matthew, we read that Jesus sent them to make disciples "of" all nations. Why nations? Nations are Jesus' inheritance. He is the King of Kings, King of all nations. He wants nations serving Him.

As previously mentioned, Jesus revealed how to disciple the nations. He said, "Go into all the world and preach the gospel to all creatures" *(Mark 16:15)*. Why would Jesus say "disciple nations" in Matthew and "world" in Mark? I thought He said, "Go around the world" and preach the gospel to every human. That is not what He told us to do. He told us to go "into" all the world.

God never sent anyone *around* the world. He always sent them *into* the world. Most of them were sent into government because He knew government was the key component that controlled every other aspect of society. If we lose our governments, eventually we will lose everything else.

We have translated this as going *around* the world because of our personal ambitions. God prepares His people and sends them into one of the components that this world is made of. I'm hoping you have already read the other volumes of the *Kingdom Awareness Series* and that you will find your calling and place.

EQUIPPING US TO FULFILL OUR DESTINY AND CALL

Once we release people into their destiny, we need to equip them with the skill and everything else they need to fulfill that destiny. The only things Jesus did not give the disciples were material things. He did not promise them any money or property. Today, that's all we give people. We bless them with material things so they do not have to trust God for anything. We do things opposite of the way Jesus did.

Almost everyone who has ever come to do ministry with me was primarily concerned with how much I was going to pay them each month. None of them remained long in the field. Jesus taught His disciples that their blessings were in the harvest they were going to bring in, not in money. Those who look for their reward before they reap any harvest will not succeed in the field. Always know that your blessing is in the harvest that will come to the kingdom through you.

The reason Jesus gave His disciples power and authority to cast out demons and heal sickness was because they needed that to fulfill the destiny He had for them. You may not need that to fulfill your destiny. You might need an education from a college or to develop a skill.

METHODS OF DISCIPLING NATIONS

THE CHURCH

It is the original plan of God to disciple nations through local churches. The church should have the vision and the heart of Jesus for the nations and their cities. The reason Jesus establishes an *ekklesia* in a city or nation is to disciple them and bring them under His Lordship. As we read in the Word, He has been waiting until all His enemies are brought to His footstool.

When we study the early church, we find that they were not having revival services every Sunday; and they were not waiting to fly away. They turned the world upside-down and then turned it back right side up the way it was supposed to be. If we look around our society, we will notice things are functioning upside-down. We are supposed to turn it back the way it's supposed to be.

The church is supposed to be equipping the saints to do the work of the ministry. Ministry is not only preaching and helping the poor.

Everything and anything a person is called by God to do is their ministry. All the methods of discipleship that are listed below should be done through the church, but today's church is limited in their vision, so God also uses parachurch organizations to do the job He always wanted to be done.

GOVERNMENTS

Church and government should never be separated. They're supposed to work in partnership. They are the two wings of the kingdom of God. One deals with the spiritual, and the other deals with the natural. They're supposed to work hand in hand to solve problems and fix what is broken.

In the Old Testament, the kings and priests worked in partnership. They were not separated and doing their own thing. They were both instrumental in discipling the nation of Israel.

One example from the early church is the evangelist, Philip, meeting the eunuch from Ethiopia. Holy Spirit told him to go to the desert of Gaza where this eunuch was traveling back to his country after visiting Jerusalem. This was not an ordinary person. He was "a eunuch of great authority under Candace, the queen of the Ethiopians, who had charge of all her treasury" *(Acts 8:27b)*.

Philip shared the gospel with him, and he was saved and baptized right there and then. He went back to Ethiopia and shared what happened to him and discipled the whole nation as a result.

AGRICULTURE

Joseph used agriculture to disciple Egypt. It was the vehicle through which He reached the entire nation. There are many countries on earth that are struggling to produce enough food for their people. As a church, we are supposed to tap into the department of agriculture in heaven and release ideas and plans to produce quality food that can feed the hungry. When a church trains its people to produce enough food for a village or a town, they are discipling that area and the people.

EDUCATION

Another method is through education. The majority of the world's political and business leaders were graduates of universities like Oxford, Yale, and Harvard. What an opportunity to shape leaders who in turn will shape the future of nations! As I mentioned earlier, the city where we are located is being discipled by a Christian school. I don't mean that they do it with that intention, but it's the result of their influence.

MEDIA

I don't need to explain much about the influence of media on our society. People wake and turn on their TVs or smartphones to see what is happening in the world. For the most part, people believe what the media says. Maybe that is changing nowadays because they have been called on for propagating "fake news." If one outlet of media is not trustworthy, people will tune in to the next one.

SCIENCE AND TECHNOLOGY

Another way to disciple a city or nation is through science and technology. We cannot emphasize the importance of them in our lives. We are very dependent on technology. Today, we can't imagine a life without it.

BUSINESS

Another effective way to disciple nations is through businesses. In many countries, there are huge businesses, which even the government

DISCOVERING PURPOSE, CALLING AND GIFTS

depends on for income. Taxes are what brings income to the government, and the more taxes citizens and companies pay, the richer the governments become.

These multinational companies literally disciple the nations they exist. People buy and depended on their products for survival. Believers need to start such companies with the intention of discipling nations.

When Joseph began to prepare Egypt for the drought, he ordered storehouses to be built in every town. Later, when the famine started, people came to him or to those storehouses to buy food. When they ran out of money, they sold their land for food. He not only used agriculture to disciple Egypt, but He used real estate and construction ventures as well. Imagine having to build storehouses through the entire land of Egypt, and how much land, materials, people, and money it took to do that. He became the wealthiest man in the whole nation, next to Pharaoh.

For example, there is a business in India that is run by a man that has had deep-rooted influence in the country for decades. They produce everything from software to salt, and I don't think there is a sector that they are not involved in. They are also the largest auto manufacturer in the whole country.

Below I've included the testimony of someone who was instrumental through business to win souls:

> "I'd like you to help us develop our marketing program beginning in January," said the CEO of a sports product company. This offer came at a time in which the consultant was delighted to have an opportunity to use his talents again. It was the first new business opportunity he'd had in some time, and he had just come out of some very difficult business and personal circumstances. A few months into

the position, the CEO asked this consultant to manage the entire marketing department, placing him over all the current marketing staff. It appeared that God was blessing his efforts with several successful initiatives. He began to build relationships with a few of the executives. One day, the sales manager came into his office and asked for help with a personal crisis. One thing led to another, and two months later, the consultant found himself leading the sales manager in the sinner's prayer in the sales manager's office.

There is not a nation that is closed to the gospel of the kingdom. We need to find out the *key* that we need to use to open the door for the gospel in each particular country. As Jesus said, He has given us the keys of His kingdom. Notice the word *key* is plural: there are many keys in a kingdom.

One of the abovementioned methods would work in every country. The problem is we have not prepared or equipped our people and released them to do it. I have heard of medical evangelism where Christian doctors dedicate their time to visit a country to donate their service and share the gospel with their patients. In the city of Philippi, Paul met a businesswoman whose heart the Lord opened to receive the gospel.

MIRACLES

I don't need to write more on this. We are all familiar with the influence that miracles have on people. Though every other method mentioned above requires the power and the wisdom of God, there are particular cases in which it manifests to surpass natural laws. We call these miracles or signs and wonders.

When we apply all the methods of discipleship mentioned above, we can reach any nation on earth within the next ten to fifteen years.

No nation is closed to the gospel of the kingdom. They are only closed to a religious gospel. May the Lord help and grant us wisdom on how to practice discipleship and on how to bring nations back to God.

FASTING AND PRAYER

When Jonah went to Nineveh to preach and announced what God was planning to do in that nation, the entire nation, from the king to animal stock, declared a three-day fast. They didn't even drink water for those three days. When they humbled themselves before God, He relented from His wrath and forgave the whole nation.

Esther and Daniel are two other examples of God using fasting and prayer to change the course of nations. We need to find out from God which method He is planning to use to disciple, change or influence a nation. He can use all of the above or just one to influence an entire nation.

I believe you have been blessed by reading this book. You may have to read it more than once to receive everything. Read it and study it until it becomes part of you. Use it for Bible study groups and teach others. When you teach something, it helps you to learn it better. To order more copies, please visit www.thekingdomnetwork.org.

I also teach a course on this book. Feel free to register for the upcoming course on our website. Thank you.

GENESIS126 PROJECT

> **Train up** a child in the way he should go, and when he is old he will not depart from it *(Proverbs 22:6)*.

How many of you wish you had raised your children a little differently than the way you did? Or wished your parents raised you differently than the way they did? We all have regrets. As parents of three teenagers, though they are wonderful, my wife and I already wish we had done some things differently when they were little. In truth, all parents wish they had another chance to raise their kids again.

If you are an adult, do you wish you had known certain things about life earlier than you did? What if you knew what you know now twenty years ago? I have heard from many people after they read one of the books this ministry publishes, saying they wished they had read that book twenty or even forty years ago. What are we going to do with our experience? Are we going to hide it because of ego or share it to make a difference for the next generation?

Our whole life hangs on three questions, and the answers to those questions determine our worldview and how we live our life. Every single person who lived on this earth is asking the same questions. Some of them found the answers, but sadly, most did not. The questions are: **Who Am I? Where Did I Come From?** and **Why Am I Here?** It is very common for me to meet believers over fifty or sixty years old and still looking for their purpose in life.

What if we had known the answers to those questions from the time we were young? What if someone had helped us find the answers to those questions? How dramatically different would our lives and the choices we made be if we had known the answers to those questions?

The biggest crisis today is the identity crisis. Young boys and girls are confused about their identity and purpose, and in some cases, even their gender. It is becoming more common for parents to allow their children to choose which gender they would like to be. The first question, "Who Am I?" deals with **IDENTITY**. The second question, "Where did I come from?" deals with our **SOURCE**. And the third, "Why Am I here?" deals with **PURPOSE**.

Knowing that every human being will ask these questions and the importance of it, God Almighty answered all of them in the very first chapter of the Bible itself. As I share in my books and teachings, Genesis 1:26 is the **purpose statement** for mankind, given by our Creator. We've neglected it, thinking it's just an Old Testament creation story.

Your spirit came into this world fully aware and with the knowledge of who you are and why you were sent to this earth. Instead of welcoming and nurturing that spirit to release what they were sent here for, most children are trained in the ways of this world. The environment in which we were born and raised plays a role in brainwashing and forming a wrong mindset in us. The sin nature we inherited plays a part in that, as well.

By His grace, the Holy Spirit has helped us find the answers and write **THREE BOOKS** to answer those questions (separate sets of books for each gender) geared toward children from 0-6 years old. They are intended to be a child's first books, and parents or grandparents will be able to read to them to instill in them the answers to those three very important questions.

God has given us the tools to raise up a new generation of **kingdom ambassadors** who will walk in their true identity and purpose and manifest the fullness of God, reclaiming the ground we lost. We are blessed to provide you with the tools you need. These books will answer those age-old questions about how to raise your children and grandchildren so they will never have to waste a day doubting who they are, why they are here, and where they came from.

They will help establish any child in their identity, purpose, and source so that when they become a teenager, they will not succumb to pressures from the culture or their peers. How many young people can you think of who have made wrong choices trying to find the answers to those three questions? It is painful, and many carry the wounds and shame of what happened in those years for the rest of their lives. Too many end their life prematurely. Teenage suicides and pregnancies are an epidemic of our day. I believe we have the solution to stop it.

Now let's look at the answers to these questions.

DISCOVERING PURPOSE, CALLING AND GIFTS

We read in Genesis 1:26, "God said, 'Let us make man in Our image and likeness and let them have dominion.'" That single line has the answers to those three questions:

- **Who Am I (Identity)?** God said, "Make man in Our image and likeness.'" I am created in the image and likeness of God; that is my identity. I am just like my heavenly Father.

- **Where did I come from (Source)?** God said, "Let Us make man," which reveals that I came from God; He is my Source.

- **Why am I here (Purpose)?** God said, "Let them have dominion." That shows my purpose.

To be born a male or a female is a natural process, but becoming a man or woman is intentional, just like no one becomes a pilot, a doctor, or a scientist by birth. They have to go through intense training to become that.

The challenge is how to practically apply those three answers to instill identity, source, and purpose into a child. What does it mean to be born in the image and likeness of God? How do we practically apply the principle of dominion and teach that to a child? This is why you need these three books. In these books, we clearly reveal the concepts (with illustrations) to minister to a child's spirit and to their soul about their identity, source, and purpose.

The first five years are the most critical years of a child's life. When a child is born, what happens to that child, what happens around them, and what they repeatedly hear is written in their brain and heart. What we put into them during those years stays in them for the rest of their life and produces fruit when they become adults.

Instead of filling their minds with movies, reading to them about animals, sports, and aliens, we need to lay the right foundation on which to build their life. Let's do a favor for our next generation so they will not make the same mistakes we made.

If we practice this **Genesis126 Project** in our homes and Sunday Schools, by the time our children are five years old, their identity as a male or a female, and the reason they are here, will be settled in them. No matter what happens to them later, they will be able to successfully navigate life.

I believe that in each successive generation, it becomes more and more challenging and difficult to raise children. The enemy is after our destiny and our children's destinies. More couples these days choose not to have any children.

As you know, children are the future of our nations. If we are going to make a difference in the future, we need to raise our children on the right foundation. That's why this program is so crucial.

God has given us the solution. Will you pray about starting a Genesis126 project for kids in your family, neighborhood, church, or anywhere it is possible? We can surely make a difference in the next generation. If we do not do anything, the enemy will continue to devour and destroy more destinies, and this world will go from bad to worse.

Will you let your light shine so that the next generation can clearly see the path they are supposed to walk? The stakes are high, and if we do not do something, the price our children will pay with their lives will be huge.

Maybe someone you know is called to minister to children. Please introduce these tools to them and spread the news. We can't be silent anymore.

Once you receive a copy of this Genesis126 project book set, you can create lessons based on each statement written in it by adding a story, activity, and its application. Keep it simple, and even if some of the things are hard for children to grasp now, the seed that will be planted into their spirit will bring forth fruit later in their lives.

To order a copy, please visit our website at
www.thekingdomnetwork.org,
or if you have more questions, feel free to email us at
info@thekingdomnetwork.org.
Thank you.

MORE BOOKS & RESOURCES

DISCIPLING NATIONS SERIES

Kingdom Mandate (for any donation)
Discovering the Lost Kingdom (Volume 1) $14.00
Purpose, Calling, and Gifts (Volume 2) $15.00
God's Original Design (Volume 3) $20.00
Seeing, Entering, and Manifesting the Kingdom of God (Volume 4)$20.00
The Ekklesia (Volume 5) $30.00
The Gospel of the Kingdom (Volume 6) $20.00
Power and Authority of the Church (Volume 7) $15.00
Kingdom Family (Volume 8) $15.00
The Birthing of a kingdom nation (Volume 9) $20.00
What Happened to God? (Volume10) $20.00
7 Dimensions and Operations of the Kingdom of God (Volume 11)$15.00
Kingdom Economy (Volume 12) $15.00
Kingdom Government (Volume 13) $15.00
Releasing Kings and Queens to their Original Intent (Volume 14) $10.00
Kingdom Secrets to Restoring Nations Back to God (Volume 15) $20.00
Keys to Fulfilling Your Kingdom Assignment (Volume 16) $15.00

KINGDOM LIVING SERIES

The Three Most Important Decisions of Your Life $15.00
Recognizing God's Timing for Your Life $12.00
Overcoming the Spirit of Poverty $10.00
Seven Kinds of Believers $10.00
7 Dimensions of God's Glory $5.00
7 Dimensions of God's Grace $10.00
7 Kinds of Faith $7.00

KINGDOM BOOKS FOR KIDS

Genesis 126 Three Volume Book set for boys $25.00

TO PLACE AN ORDER:

www.TheKingdomNetwork.org
Phone: 1-800-558-5020
Email: info@TheKingdomNetwork.org

Are you struggling to discover your **PURPOSE ?**
You are not supposed to fit in but stand out !

Sign up today for the upcoming FREE Online Kingdom Course

DISCOVERING THE LOST KINGDOM

In this course you'll DISCOVER:

- Your true identity and purpose
- What God is doing on the earth and how you can partner with Him in it
- Why God created the earth and put us on this planet

  And much more ...

Why are people becoming more and more disinterested in **church and religion** globally?
Join the course, and discover **what your soul has been searching for all along.**

FREE BOOK AND STUDY GUIDE

other courses available
- DISCOVERING PURPOSE, CALLING AND GIFTS
- SEEING, ENTERING AND MANIFESTING THE KINGDOM
- GOD'S ORIGINAL DESIGN | FEBRUARY 2024
- The Ekklesia
- The Next move of GOD

  And more ...

Register Now @ **www.TheKingdomUniversity.org**

Welcome to

KINGDOM DELIVERANCE
— WORKSHOP —

Are you tired of waiting and looking for breakthroughs? Kingdom of God has the answer.

This kingdom deconstruct workshop is divided into EIGHT major categories which deal with the seven major areas of our life. Each one is connected to the next, and so if one of these areas dysfunctions, it will affect all other areas of your life.

1. Relationship with the Father
2. Spiritual Healing
3. Emotional Healing
4. Recognizing Purpose and Calling
5. Identifying and Mastering Natural and Spiritual Gifts
6. Finances—Learning to Live in Kingdom Economy
7. Healing Relationships
8. Physical Health

Take action now. Order all 8 workshop manuals today!

Thank you so much for taking the courses from The Kingdom University. Taking a course is only the first step. We are pleased to present you with the next step—that of going through the process to get rid of all the extra weights that have been slowing and hindering you from fully living out your kingdom assignment.

Call 1 800 558 5020   www.TheKingdomNetwork.org

www.ingramcontent.com/pod-product-compliance
Lightning Source LLC
Chambersburg PA
CBHW070134080526
44586CB00015B/1682